Practice B

4

CENTER STAGE

Express Yourself in English

Lynn Bonesteel
Samuela Eckstut-Didier

Series Consultants
MaryAnn Florez Sharon Seymour

PEARSON
Longman

Center Stage 4: Express Yourself in English
Practice Book

Pearson Education, 10 Bank Street, White Plains, NY 10606

Staff credits: The people who made up the **Center Stage 4 Practice Book** team, representing editorial, production, design, and manufacturing are Pietro Alongi, Wendy Campbell, Diane Cipollone, Dave Dickey, Warren Fischbach, Aliza Greenblatt, Ray Keating, and Melissa Leyva.

Text composition: ElectraGraphics, Inc.

Text font: 9.5/11 Minion Pro

Photo credits: p. 79 © Vincent Laforet/Pool/Reuters/Corbis; **p. 84** Medio Images/AgeFotoStock

Illustration Credits: A Corazon Abierto (Marcela Gomez), Steve Attoe, Laurie A. Conley, Debby Fisher, Marty Harris, John Kanzler, Luis Montiel, Francisco Morales, Chris Pavely, Mari Rodriguez, Roberto Sadi, John Schreiner, Steve Schulman, Gary Torrisi, Meryl Treatner

ISBN-13: 978-0-13-607019-1
ISBN-10: 0-13-607019-1

Pearsonlongman on the Web
Pearsonlongman.com offers online resources for teachers and students.
Access our Companion Websites, our online catalog, and our local offices around the world.
Visit us at **pearsonlongman.com.**

Printed in the United States of America

1 2 3 4 5 6 7 8 9 10—BR—12 11 10 09 08

Contents

Unit 1 1
Unit 2 6
Unit 3 12
Unit 4 18
Unit 5 23
Unit 6 28
Unit 7 33
Unit 8 38
Unit 9 43
Unit 10 48
Unit 11 54
Unit 12 59
Unit 13 64
Unit 14 69
Unit 15 74
Unit 16 79
Unit 17 84
Unit 18 89
Unit 19 94
Unit 20 100
Answer Key 105

NAME: ______________________________ DATE: ____________

UNIT 1 VOCABULARY EXERCISE

Complete the diary entry. Use the words in the box.

appeared	direct	perform	win awards
be in the competition	get a part	~~try out for~~	

Middleton High School has a fantastic theater department. Every year, the school has a talent show. Many students try out for (1.) the show. Some students dance, and some sing. Other students do magic tricks or tell jokes. If the performers are good, they __________ (2.) in the show. About 30 performers are chosen each year. On the night of the show, the students __________ (3.) for an audience of more than 300 people. They're nervous! It's exciting to __________ (4.), but it's also scary! The best three performers __________ (5.).

Last year, I __________ (6.) in the show. I was very nervous, and I forgot the words to my song. I'm not a very good performer! I love the theater, but I don't want to perform. Next year, I think I'll __________ (7.) a play. On opening night, I can sit in the audience and watch other people perform.

NAME: ______________________ DATE: ______________

UNIT 1 GRAMMAR EXERCISES

Grammar to Communicate 1: Present Perfect

Complete each sentence. Circle the correct answer.

1. My sister **tried out** / **has tried out** for a part in the school play last Friday.
2. I **performed** / **have performed** in several piano competitions, and my next one is on Sunday.
3. Johnny Depp **appeared** / **has appeared** in a lot of good movies.
4. Princess Diana **received** / **has received** several awards for helping people before she died.
5. My boyfriend **didn't call** / **hasn't called** me yesterday, and I'm a little worried.
6. John and I **knew** / **have known** each other for ten years, and I think we'll always be friends.
7. I **was never** / **have never been** in a competition before—I'm really nervous.

B **Complete the sentences. Write the correct form of the verbs. Use the present perfect or the simple past.**

1. Audrey Hepburn ___was___ (be) a very stylish actress. She __________ (make) *Breakfast at Tiffany's* in 1961. It __________ (be) one of her best movies.
2. The children __________ (practice) the holiday song every day last week. Their performance last night __________ (be) excellent.
3. Our class __________ (make) three short films this year. We __________ (finish) our third film last week, and we're starting our next one tomorrow.
4. I __________ (be) to Hollywood twice. I __________ (see) a lot of movie stars on my last visit.

NAME: ______________________________ DATE: ____________

Grammar to Communicate 2: Present Perfect and Simple Past (I)

A **Complete the sentences. Write the correct form of the verbs. Use the present perfect or the simple past.**

1. Tom Cruise has been (be) an actor since he __________ (be) a young man. He __________ (perform) in many movies.
2. Manny __________ (join) a new band last week. He __________ (play) with three different groups since high school. He __________ (be) a drummer for more than ten years.
3. Mr. and Mrs. Acosta __________ (be) together for many years. They __________ (get) married in 1983, but they __________ (know) each other since 1977.
4. Andy and Sam __________ (meet) to play tennis every Saturday morning since they __________ (be) teenagers. Since they __________ (start) playing together, both of them __________ (become) excellent players.

B **Complete the sentences. Use *for* or *since*.**

1. Rob has played professional baseball since 2003.
2. Maryanne and Brian have been dance partners __________ twelve years.
3. I've played the violin __________ almost six years—__________ I was fourteen.
4. Hip-hop music has been popular __________ many years.
5. Silvia has taught at the art school __________ 2006.
6. *The Sound of Music* has been a popular movie __________ it was first released in 1965.
7. The Rolling Stones have entertained their fans __________ over 40 years.

NAME: ______________________________ DATE: ______________

Grammar to Communicate 3: Present Perfect and Simple Past (2)

A **Complete each sentence. Circle the letter of the correct answer.**

1. I've played on a basketball team ______.

   a. when I was in high school (b.) since I was 17 years old

2. Have you ever ______ a dance class?

   a. take b. taken

3. What movies ______ so far this year?

   a. have you seen b. did you see

4. I've lost twelve pounds since I ______ the gym last year.

   a. joined b. 've joined

5. My mother has been an Elton John fan for ______.

   a. a very long time b. more than twenty years ago

B **Complete the conversation. Use the simple past or the present perfect of the verbs.**

Jim: Have you ever been (1. (you / ever / be)) to Hollywood?

Sara: Yes. ____________ (2. (I / be)) there twice.

Jim: When ____________ (3. (you / go))?

Sara: The first time, ____________ (4. (I / go)) with my family. ____________ (5. (I / be)) only four years old. The second time ____________ (6. (be)) last year. ____________ (7. (I / do)) all the fun touristy things. And ____________ (8. (I / see)) Cameron Diaz on Rodeo Drive. ____________ (9. (She / always / be)) my favorite movie star. ____________ (10. (you / ever / see)) any of her movies?

Jim: ____________ (11. (I / see)) only a few of her movies, but I like her, too.

NAME: ______________________________ DATE: ______________

Review and Challenge

Correct the e-mail. There are nine mistakes. The first one is corrected for you.

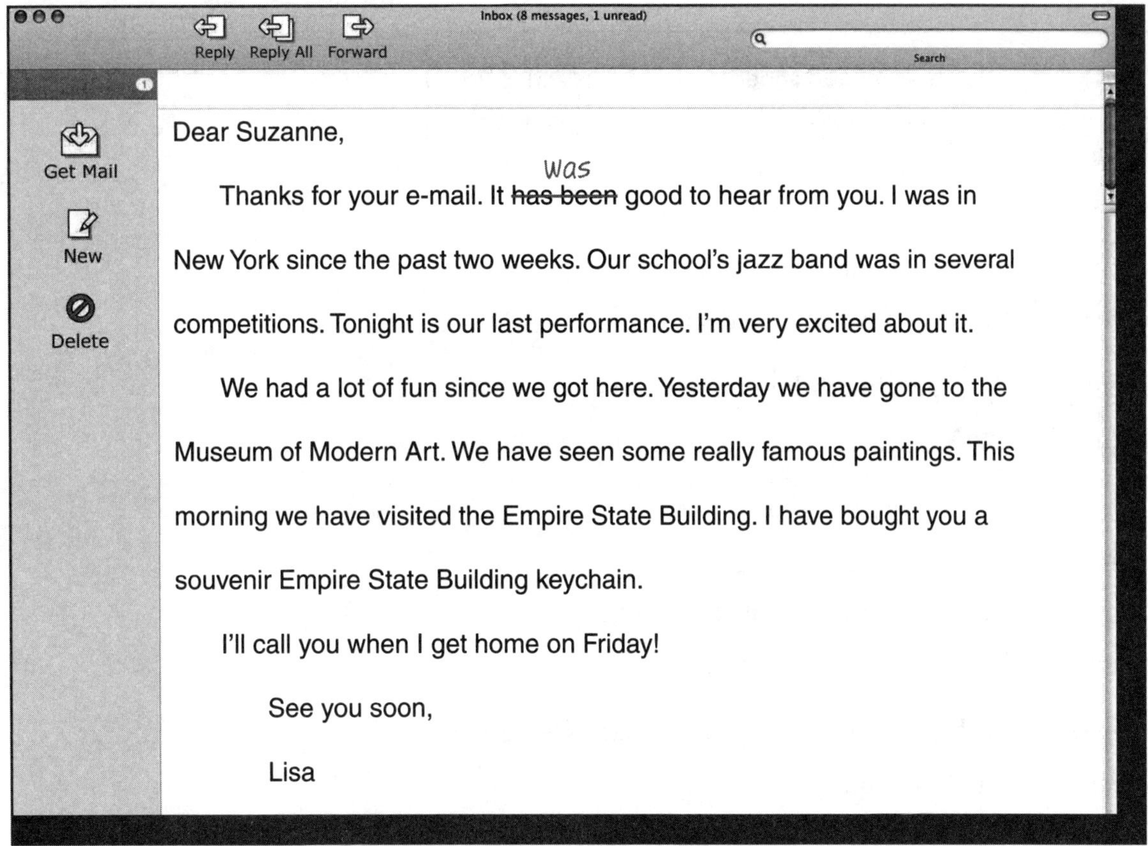

Dear Suzanne,

Thanks for your e-mail. It ~~has been~~ was good to hear from you. I was in New York since the past two weeks. Our school's jazz band was in several competitions. Tonight is our last performance. I'm very excited about it.

We had a lot of fun since we got here. Yesterday we have gone to the Museum of Modern Art. We have seen some really famous paintings. This morning we have visited the Empire State Building. I have bought you a souvenir Empire State Building keychain.

I'll call you when I get home on Friday!

See you soon,

Lisa

NAME: ______________________________ DATE: ______________

UNIT 2 VOCABULARY EXERCISE

Complete the conversations. Use the words in the box.

arthritis	have a good appetite	is acting up
chicken pox	have trouble sleeping	~~painkillers~~
diabetes	injury	vitamins

1. **Patient:** I have a terrible headache.
   Doctor: It's a migraine. You need some ____painkillers____.
2. **Patient:** My fingers hurt when I move them.
   Doctor: That's __________________ in your hands.
3. **John:** Why are you so tired?
   Carlos: I __________________.
   John: Are you worried about something?
   Carlos: I'm worried about everything!
4. **Mother:** My daughter is sick. Can the doctor see her today?
   Nurse: What's wrong?
   Mother: She has a fever, and there are red spots on her skin.
   Nurse: I think that's __________________. Bring her to the office this morning.
5. **Ulma:** Is Jessica playing in the basketball game?
   Andrea: No, she hurt her ankle. It's a very bad __________________.
6. **Doctor:** I have bad news, Mr. Wang. You have to be careful about your diet. No more sugar!
   Mr. Wang: But I love cakes, cookies, and pies. I'm a baker.
   Doctor: You have __________________. That's a serious disease.
7. **Dad:** Who wants more chicken and potatoes?
   Angelo: I do.
   Dad: Well, I see you __________________.

8. **Eiko:** I have no energy. I'm always tired.

Eriko: Do you eat a healthy diet?

Eiko: Well, not really. I'm busy, and I don't always have time to eat.

Eriko: Maybe you need some ____________________.

9. **Jean-Paul:** My back hurts. My old injury ____________________ again.

Doctor: You have to rest. At your age, you can't play tennis every day.

NAME: ______________________________ DATE: ______________

UNIT 2 GRAMMAR EXERCISES

Grammar to Communicate 1: Present Perfect Progressive

A **Complete the sentences. Use the present perfect progressive form of the verbs.**

1. I 've been waiting (wait) for the doctor for almost an hour.
2. Tomas ________ (study) medicine for six years.
3. Dr. Sala ________ (examine) a patient since early this morning.
4. The patient ________ (complain) about a stomachache since he arrived.
5. I ________ (not / cry). My eyes are red because I have allergies.
6. My sister and I ________ (take) allergy medications since we were little.

B **Complete the conversations. Use the present perfect progressive. Add *not* where necessary.**

1. **A:** Would you like some cake for dessert?

   B: No, thank you. I have been trying (try) to watch my weight lately. I ________ (eat) anything fattening these days—just salad and vegetables.

2. **A:** Is your mother okay? She looks like she is in pain.

   B: Her arthritis ________ (act up) over the past few days. She says her fingers ________ (hurt) a lot.

3. **A:** You ________ (cough) all morning. Do you have a cold?

   B: Yes, a bad one. I ________ (feel) well since Monday.

4. **A:** Did I wake you?

   B: Yes, but it's OK. I ________ (take) some strong painkillers for my back, and they ________ (make) me really sleepy. I was just taking a little nap.

NAME: ______________________________ DATE: ______________

Grammar to Communicate 2: Present Perfect Progressive and Present Perfect (I)

A **Complete the stories. Use the present perfect or the present perfect progressive. There may be more than one correct answer.**

Sam ___has had___ (1. have) asthma since he was a child. He ________________ (2. take) medication for it for years. He took his medication this morning, but he ________________ (3. cough) all day. And he ________________ (4. have) trouble breathing.

Donna ________________ (5. go) to Dr. Soto since she was a teenager. He ________________ (6. be) her doctor for a very long time. Dr. Soto gave Donna some tests earlier in the week because she ________________ (7. not / feel) well lately. She ________________ (8. wait) to hear the results, and she ________________ (9. feel) a little nervous all day. Dr. Soto's office ________________ (10. not / call) yet, and it's almost 5:00.

B **Correct the conversations. There is one mistake in each conversation.**

1. **A:** Why is your face so red?
   B: I've ~~exercised~~ been exercising for the last 45 minutes.
2. **A:** Have you been finishing last night's homework?
   B: What homework?
3. **A:** Have you been going to the hospital yet to see Hannah and her new baby?
   B: No. I've been working all day, and now visiting hours have ended!
4. **A:** My surgeon has been doing this operation for years.
   B: That's good. I've been being a little worried about you.
5. **A:** Have you ever been having the chicken pox?
   B: No. I don't think I ever had it as a child.

NAME: ______________________________ DATE: ______________

Grammar to Communicate 3: Present Perfect Progressive and Present Perfect (2)

A **Complete each sentence. Circle the correct answer.**

1. The game has been going on for an hour, and **the score is 4–4** / **the score was 8–6.**
2. The game has ended, and **the score is 4–4 / the score was 8–6.**
3. They've played soccer **every day this week / since 11:00 this morning.**
4. I've been taking tennis lessons **for about a year / last year.**
5. I've been drinking four cups of coffee **today / every day.**
6. Our team has been playing **two games / for almost an hour.**

B **Write the questions. Use the present perfect or the present perfect progressive.**

1. How many times / you / exercise / this week

   How many times have you exercised this week?

2. How long / you / study / at this school

   ____

3. How many times / you / go / to the doctor / so far this year

   ____

4. How much water / you / drink / today

   ____

5. How many colds / you / have / so far this year

   ____

6. How long / you / work / on this exercise

   ____

NAME: ______________________________ DATE: ______________

Review and Challenge

Correct the letter. There are seven mistakes. The first mistake is corrected for you.

Dear Jennifer,

Do you remember that I had a doctor's appointment last week? Well, I've just received ~~been receiving~~ an upsetting phone call. Dr. Grey's office called to tell me that my test results aren't very good. I was really surprised to hear this because I've been trying really hard to get in better shape. I've been eating healthier food, and I've taken long walks several times a week. This week, I've been taking a walk every day!

The doctor says that I am 25 pounds overweight and that I might get diabetes! I can't believe it! But I have to believe it. After all, Dr. Grey has been knowing me almost all my life. So I've been deciding to do something about it. I've gone through all the food in my kitchen, and I've thrown away all the junk food. And I've been calling health clubs for the past few hours. I haven't been found one yet, but I'll keep trying. Have you ever been belonging to a gym? All the gyms I've called so far are really expensive!

Love, Monica

NAME: ______________________ DATE: ______________

UNIT 3 VOCABULARY EXERCISES

Read the police report. Then complete each sentence. Circle the correct word.

POLICE REPORT

On December 31st, Mr. and Mrs. Green came home and found their door open. A chocolate cake in the kitchen was gone, and there were empty milk bottles on the kitchen table. A neighbor, Luis Alvarez, said that he saw two teenagers in the yard around eight o'clock. Police officer Tim Wang asked Mr. Alvarez to describe the teenagers. Mr. Alvarez said they looked hungry.

1. The crime is a __________.
   - (break-in)
   - murder
2. Mr. and Mrs. Green are the __________.
   - suspects
   - victims
   - witnesses
3. Mr. Alvarez is a __________.
   - suspect
   - victim
   - witness
4. Two teenagers are the __________.
   - suspects
   - victims
   - witnesses
5. Tim Wang __________ Mr. Alvarez.
   - investigated
   - questioned
6. Tim Wang __________ the crime.
   - investigated
   - questioned
7. Tim Wang is probably a __________.
   - detective
   - robber

B **Look at the picture. Read the police report. Then complete each sentence. Circle the letter of the correct answer.**

POLICE REPORT

At 2:30 today, two men with guns walked into a convenience store and demanded all the money in the cash register. The cash register had only $50. The men became angry and demanded the cashier's watch. At that moment, a police officer came into the store to buy donuts. He caught the men. One of the suspects was later identified as Gerald Jones. The police know Jones had robbed other stores. They now suspect that he also killed a man.

1. The crime is a __________.

   a. break-in **b.** robbery **c.** murder

2. Gerald Jones was one of the __________.

   a. robbers **b.** victims **c.** witnesses

3. After __________, police found out that Jones had robbed other stores.

   a. a question **b.** a detective **c.** an investigation

4. The police think Gerald Jones committed a __________.

   a. break-in **b.** murder **c.** victim

NAME: ______________________ DATE: ______________

UNIT 3 GRAMMAR EXERCISES

Grammar to Communicate 1: Past Perfect

A **Complete the story. Use the past perfect form of the verbs.**

Before today's break-in, I ___had loved___ (1. love) living in my apartment. I ______________ (2. feel) very safe and comfortable. There ______________ (3. never / be) a crime in my building before today. It ______________ (4. be) a safe place to live.

Luckily, I wasn't home when the burglar broke into my apartment. I ______________ (5. leave) for work a few hours before. By the time I got home, the police ______________ (6. arrive). When they questioned my neighbors, one of them said she ______________ (7. see) a young man looking in my window earlier in the day. When she saw him again later, she called the police. But she ______________ (8. call) too late. By the time the police arrived, the man ______________ (9. get) away and my new CD player ______________ (10. disappear).

B **Write sentences. Put the words in the correct order. Use the past perfect form of the verbs.**

1. by Sunday afternoon / The police / arrest / a suspect

   The police had arrested a suspect by Sunday afternoon.

2. The man / two stores / and three houses / rob

   ____

3. By Saturday night, / question / the police / four witnesses

   ____

4. see / One witness / the suspect / clearly

   ____

5. by Sunday night / The detectives / find / the stolen money

   ____

NAME: ______________________ DATE: ______________

Grammar to Communicate 2: Past Perfect and Simple Past

Complete the stories. Use the simple past or past perfect of the verbs.

I ___had been___ (1. be) home for almost an hour before I ______ (2. see) the broken window. I ______ (3. not / notice) it sooner because I ______ (4. not / go) into the bedroom. My husband ______ (5. not / come) home from work yet, so I ______ (6. be) alone in the house. When I ______ (7. call) the police, they ______ (8. tell) me to lock the doors and wait for them. By the time the police ______ (9. arrive), I ______ (10. discover) that all of my jewelry was gone. The robber ______ (11. also / take) my husband's DVD collection that he ______ (12. have) since he was a child.

My friend Sal and I ______ (13. be) in the bank for just a few minutes when we ______ (14. hear) someone scream. A man with a gun ______ (15. come) into the bank, and he was pointing the gun at the bank manager. When I ______ (16. look) at the man, I knew I ______ (17. see) him before. All of a sudden, I ______ (18. remember) where I ______ (19. see) him. He ______ (20. live) next door to me when I ______ (21. be) in college. His name was Bill Collier. "When ______ he ______ (22. become) a bank robber?" I thought. The bank manager ______ (23. give) him some money, and Bill ______ (24. run) out of the bank. He ______ (25. already / drive) away when the police ______ (26. arrive). Thanks to the information I gave them, the police ______ (27. already / arrest) Bill by the end of the day. Poor Bill!

NAME: ______________________ DATE: ______________

Grammar to Communicate 3: Past Perfect Progressive

A **Complete the story. Use the past progressive or the past perfect progressive form of the verbs.**

It was almost 9:00, and Dean and Doris ___were lying___ (1. lie) under a bed in the furniture department at Stacy's Department Store. They ______________ (2. lie) there for almost an hour. They ______________ (3. wait) for the store to close. They ______________ (4. plan) this robbery for a year, and they didn't want anything to go wrong. When the store was empty, they were going to load up the truck that ______________ (5. wait) for them behind the store. But suddenly, someone said "Come out of there, please." It was the store security guard. He ______________ (6. watch) Dean and Doris since they came into the store and he had seen them crawl under the bed to hide. Thieves ______________ (7. try) this since the store opened almost 50 years ago. The security guard ______________ (8. not / work) at Stacy's for very long, but Dean and Doris weren't the first thieves he'd caught. At 9:30 Dean, Doris, and the security guard ______________ (9. wait) for the police. They ______________ (10. wait) less than ten minutes before the police arrived. This isn't the ending that Dean and Doris ______________ (11. expect).

B **Complete the sentences. Use the correct verb forms.**

1. The burglar entered the apartment building at 9:30 P.M. Someone ___had left___ (leave) the front door open.
2. Before he __________ (get) in, he __________ (watch) the building for two hours.
3. I __________ (watch) TV when I __________ (hear) someone at the door.
4. I knew someone __________ (try) to get into my apartment, so I __________ (scream), "Go away!" and then I __________ (call) the police.
5. When the police __________ (arrest) the man, he admitted that he __________ (break) into apartments for years.

NAME: ______________________ DATE: ____________

Review and Challenge

Find the mistake in each item. Circle the letter and correct the mistake.

1. Yesterday was (A) my first driving lesson. I had (B) never drive (C) a car before (D).
   Correct: driven

2. There was (A) a carjacking in my neighborhood yesterday, but the police had already (B) been arresting (C) a suspect by (D) last night.
   Correct: ______________________

3. We hadn't (A) been living (B) in our house for very long when (C) someone had broken (D) in.
   Correct: ______________________

4. By (A) the time (B) the police arrived (C), the thief got (D) away.
   Correct: ______________________

5. We had been (A) waiting (B) for almost an hour before (C) the police had come (D).
   Correct: ______________________

6. While we had been waiting (A) for the police, we made (B) a list of all the things the thief had (C) stolen (D).
   Correct: ______________________

7. We were (A) all feeling (B) very upset because we had (C) been losing (D) some of our favorite things.
   Correct: ______________________

8. The police officers told (A) us that there had been (B) two break-ins on our street in the past week; no one told (C) us that before (D).
   Correct: ______________________

9. I had (A) never been (B) a crime victim, but my wife was (C) the victim of a pickpocket when she had lived (D) in New York.
   Correct: ______________________

10. She was living (A) in the city for (B) many years before that happened (C), and she had always (D) felt very safe.
    Correct: ______________________

NAME: ______________________ DATE: ______________

UNIT 4 VOCABULARY EXERCISE

Complete the conversation. Use the words in the box.

~~complex~~	garbage disposal	landlord	superintendent	trash chute
entrance	landlady	security guard	tenant	

Tuan: How's your new apartment?

Luz: It's OK. It's in a large apartment ___complex___ (1.).

Tuan: Is the apartment modern?

Luz: Oh, yes! The kitchen is really nice. There's a new oven and a new refrigerator. There's also a new ______________ (2.) under the sink.

Tuan: How's the rent?

Luz: Not too bad. And I don't have to pay for water or electricity. They're included.

Tuan: What floor are you on?

Luz: I'm on the ninth floor.

Tuan: You have a long walk to take out the garbage!

Luz: Not at all. There's a ______________ (3.) at the end of the hall.

Tuan: So you haven't had any problems yet?

Luz: Well, I had a broken window, but I called the ______________ (4.) and he came up and fixed it the next day.

Tuan: Have you met your neighbors yet?

Luz: Only the ______________ (5.) next door. She has two children. So, do you want to come over and see the apartment?

Tuan: Sure. I'm looking for a better place to live. Can I get the name of your ______________ (6.) or ______________ (7.)?

Luz: Of course. The company is Woodside Management. There's a security desk at the ______________ (8.) of the complex. Give your name to the ______________ (9.), and then go to Building C. Their office is number 110.

NAME: ______________________________ DATE: ______________

UNIT 4 GRAMMAR EXERCISES

Grammar to Communicate I: Indefinite and Definite Articles (I)

A **Which sentence does the speaker say first? Write *1* (first) and *2* (second).**

1. a. __1__ There is an apartment available at this complex.
   b. __2__ The apartment is on the second floor of the building.
2. a. ____ The stove is electric.
   b. ____ There is a new stove in the kitchen.
3. a. ____ The balcony in this apartment has a view of the water.
   b. ____ All the apartments have balconies.
4. a. ____ A superintendent lives in all the buildings.
   b. ____ The superintendents are very friendly.
5. a. ____ We don't have a key for our mailbox.
   b. ____ We should ask the landlord for the key.

B **Complete the letter. Add the appropriate article. If no article is necessary, write Ø.**

Dear Laurie,

I'm writing with exciting news: I've just moved into __a__ (1.) new apartment downtown. ______ (2.) building is on Main Street, across from ______ (3.) post office. It's ______ (4.) really nice building, and I love my apartment. There are ______ (5.) huge windows with ______ (6.) views of the river. ______ (7.) views are really beautiful at night. My apartment is on ______ (8.) tenth floor, but there's ______ (9.) elevator. ______ (10.) elevator is one of those modern high-speed elevators. It's very fast. ______ (11.) building also has ______ (12.) swimming pool. ______ (13.) pool is on the roof, and it's open until 11:00 P.M. Can you come for ______ (14.) visit next week? Call me!

Love, Julie

NAME: ______________________________ DATE: ______________

Grammar to Communicate 2: Indefinite and Definite Articles (2)

A **Read the conversations. Answer the question about each conversation. Write *yes* or *no*.**

1. **A:** The light isn't working.
   B: I'll call the superintendent.
   Is there more than one light? __No__
2. **A:** A light is out.
   B: We need to complain to the landlord.
   Is there more than one light? ____
3. **A:** Would you hang up this picture for me?
   B: Sure. Just give me the hammer and a nail.
   Do they have more than one hammer? ____
4. **A:** Where can we put all these dirty clothes?
   B: We should use some trash bags.
   Are trash bags in the same room? ____

B **Complete the conversation. Write *a, an, some, any,* or *the*.**

A: Could you give me __an__ (1.) application form, please?

B: Sure. Are you interested in renting or in buying ____ (2.) apartment?

A: I'd like to rent ____ (3.) nice apartment downtown. I really like ____ (4.) building on ____ (5.) corner of First Avenue and Main Street. It's ____ (6.) beautiful building.

B: Yes, it is. Let me see if there are ____ (7.) empty apartments in that building. . . . OK. Yes, there are ____ (8.) apartments available there. There's ____ (9.) small apartment on ____ (10.) first floor, and there's ____ (11.) larger apartment on ____ (12.) third floor.

A: Great! Can I look at ____ (13.) apartments today?

B: Of course. I just need ____ (14.) information about you first. Then we can take ____ (15.) number 6 bus downtown.

NAME: ________________________________ DATE: ______________

Grammar to Communicate 3: Generic Nouns

A **Rewrite the sentences. Make the underlined words plural and change the verb forms where necessary.**

1. We've always lived in an apartment.

   We've always lived in apartments.

2. An apartment is usually easier than a house.

   ____

3. In an apartment building, a superintendent does the tenants' repairs.

   ____

4. A house is expensive to keep up.

   ____

5. When you live in an apartment, a neighbor is always close by.

   ____

B **Complete the sentences. Use *a*, *an*, or *the*. If no article is necessary, write Ø. Capitalize letters where necessary.**

1. __Ø__ ~~l~~L ocation is very important to most people.
2. ______ apartment is usually less expensive to live in than a house.
3. Ravenna is ______ very safe neighborhood.
4. People don't have to worry about ______ crime in Ravenna.
5. People who live downtown usually take ______ public transportation.
6. I live in ______ tall white building next to ______ post office on 3rd Street.
7. I prefer wood floors to ______ carpeting.
8. ______ good schools are important to ______ couple that lives next door to me. They have ______ four-year-old daughter.

NAME: ______________________ DATE: ______________

Review and Challenge

Find and correct the mistake in each item. The first one is corrected for you.

1. Many people like living in ~~the~~ apartments. They think an apartment is easier than a house.
2. Do you know where a superintendent is? He was supposed to be here an hour ago!
3. I want to buy some new curtains. I don't like curtains that I have now.
4. Let's meet at a coffee shop on the ground floor of your building.
5. I think there might be the apartment available next month.
6. I don't have some extra keys for my apartment. Can you make one for me later today?
7. A dishwasher isn't working, and the garbage disposal is making a terrible noise.
8. A parking is sometimes hard to find in my neighborhood.
9. Tenants pay rent, and the landlords should take care of their buildings.
10. Peter has the very noisy neighbors.

NAME: ______________________________ DATE: ______________

UNIT 5 VOCABULARY EXERCISE

Match the questions with the answers. Write the correct letters.

__d__ **1.** Do you think Janice will move up in the company?

____ **2.** Where is Mrs. Hill's new work area?

____ **3.** Did you see the applicant's references?

____ **4.** Does Ana type 50 words a minute and have two years of office experience?

____ **5.** Did Francesca ask to work from 10 A.M. to 6 P.M.?

____ **6.** Why is Lin going to work in sales?

____ **7.** Did Mr. Lu offer the sales job to Lin?

____ **8.** Does Eriko know how to use the new copy machine?

____ **9.** Did Jean need directions to the office?

____ **10.** Is the boss happy with Natalie's work?

a. She's in the cubicle by the copy machine.

b. She has the right personality. She's energetic and friendly.

c. Yes, she did. She's not from around here.

d. Yes. I'm sure she's going to get a promotion this year.

e. Yes. He asked her if she wanted the job yesterday and she accepted it.

f. Yes, she meets those qualifications.

g. Yes. She gave me the names and contact information of all her previous employers.

h. Yes. He thinks her job performance is excellent.

i. Yes. Her supervisor told her the company policies allow flexible hours.

j. Yes. She's familiar with it.

NAME: ______________________ DATE: ______________

UNIT 5 GRAMMAR EXERCISES

Grammar to Communicate 1: Tag Questions

A **Complete the questions. Use tag questions.**

1. This isn't your first job, _____is it?_____
2. You drove to work today, ______________
3. Brian can't type, ______________
4. You're going to Annette's party after work on Friday, ______________
5. This office has a nice view, ______________
6. You haven't met the new boss, ______________
7. He's from around here, ______________
8. She won't ask us to work late again tonight, ______________

B **Read the questions. Rewrite them as tag questions.**

1. Are you going to check all the applicants' references?
   You're going to check all the applicants' references, aren't you?
2. Have you interviewed more than one applicant for the job?
   ____
3. Is there another applicant waiting in the reception area?
   ____
4. Should you spend more than five minutes with each applicant?
   ____
5. Did you tell the receptionist to offer the applicants coffee?
   ____
6. Will you make your decision by the end of the week?
   ____

NAME: ______________________________ DATE: ______________

Grammar to Communicate 2: *So / Too / Either / Neither*

Complete the conversations. Write *either, neither, so,* or *too*. Capitalize letters where necessary.

1. **A:** I've never worked for a large company.

   B: I haven't ___either___.

2. **A:** I have an interview tomorrow afternoon.

   B: You're kidding! __________ do I.

3. **A:** I bought a new suit for my interview.

   B: I did, __________. It's gray.

4. **A:** I'm not going to wear a tie to the interview.

   B: __________ am I. I hate ties!

5. **A:** I won't be able to sleep very well tonight.

   B: I won't __________. I never can sleep before an interview.

B **Two people are having trouble at work. Write the responses.**

1. **A:** My computer froze twice yesterday.

   B: ___Mine did, too.___ (too)

2. **A:** I never have time to finish my work.

   B: ______________________ (either)

3. **A:** My chair isn't comfortable.

   B: ______________________ (neither)

4. **A:** I haven't taken any vacation.

   B: ______________________ (neither)

5. **A:** I'm tired of working long hours.

   B: ______________________ (too)

6. **A:** My head hurts.

   B: ______________________ (too)

7. **A:** My eyes are tired.

   B: ______________________ (so)

8. **A:** I didn't get a promotion.

   B: ______________________ (either)

NAME: ______________________________ DATE: ______________

Grammar to Communicate 3: *Both . . . And / Either . . . Or / Neither . . . Nor*

A **Complete the sentences. Use *both . . . and, either . . . or,* or *neither . . . nor.* Capitalize letters where necessary.**

1. Neither the receptionist nor the office manager came to work today. Who's going to answer the phone?
2. The company is on the second floor. We can take __________ the elevator __________ the stairs.
3. There's __________ coffee __________ tea down the hall. Help yourself!
4. It's been a terrible year at my company. The employees have received __________ promotions __________ raises.
5. This job requires __________ a college degree __________ work experience. It will be hard to find someone with those qualifications, won't it?
6. The applicants will find out the company's decision __________ Friday __________ Monday—probably Monday.

B **Complete each sentence. Circle the correct answer.**

1. Either the president or the executive director **needs / need** to sign this.
2. Both the restroom and the public phone **is / are** located down the hall.
3. Neither a photocopy nor a fax **is / are** acceptable. We require the original document.
4. Either Ms. Costa or Mr. Deng **is / are** moving up. We haven't decided who.
5. Both Joe and Pat **has / have** applied for a new job.
6. Neither Joe nor Pat **thinks / think** they'll get the position.

NAME: ______________________________ DATE: ______________

Review and Challenge

Find and correct the mistake in each conversation.

1. **A:** I started working here last month.
   So did I. / I did, too.
   B: ~~I did so.~~

2. **A:** I'll have Friday nights off, haven't I?

   B: Yes.

3. **A:** You couldn't drive me to the airport tomorrow, couldn't you?

   B: Sorry, I'll be busy then.

4. **A:** They offered you the job, did they?

   B: Yes.

5. **A:** I didn't get a copy of the company's policies.

   B: I didn't neither.

6. **A:** Either a college degree or a lot of experience are needed to get that job.

   B: Really?

7. **A:** I want to either work for a large international company and start my own business. I can't decide.

   B: That's a tough decision.

8. **A:** Both talent and creativity is required for this position.

   B: Well, I'm talented and creative!

9. **A:** Jane has a great personality, does she?

   B: Oh, yes. She's a wonderful person.

10. **A:** You aren't going to be here tomorrow, will you?

    B: No. I have to visit my mother.

NAME: ______________________________ DATE: ______________

UNIT 6 VOCABULARY EXERCISE

Complete the sentences. Use the words in the box.

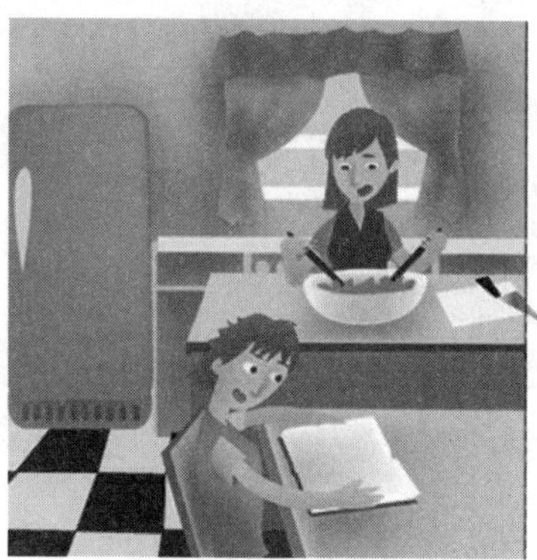

~~boil~~	consume	cultivate	invented	steam
broil	create	fry	marinate	

1. Alicia put a large pot of water on the stove. She's going to ____boil____ water to cook potatoes.
2. Jorge put a little butter in a pan. He's going to ________________ eggs for breakfast.
3. The secret is to ________________ the chicken in lemon, garlic, salt, and pepper for about four hours before you cook it.
4. Lenore placed the steak under the heat. She's going to ________________ the meat.
5. Thomas Sullivan ________________ tea bags in 1908. He made the tea bags from silk.
6. People began to ________________ plants for food as early as 8000 B.C.
7. People in New Zealand ________________ more ice cream per person than any other country.
8. To ________________ vegetables, place the vegetables in a metal container above boiling water.
9. With a few basic ingredients, you can ________________ delicious meals.

NAME: ______________________ DATE: ____________

UNIT 6 GRAMMAR EXERCISES

Grammar to Communicate 1: Simple Present: Passive

A **Complete the sentences. Use the passive form.**

1. Ceviche __is served__ (serve) all over Central and South America.
2. To make ceviche, raw fish ________ (marinate) in lime juice for several hours.
3. Tomatoes, onions, and peppers ________ (add) to the fish before it ________ (eat).
4. Most cookies ________ (bake) in the oven for about 15 minutes.
5. A popular type of cookie that ________ (sell) in many parts of the world is the chocolate-chip cookie.
6. How many chocolate-chip cookies ________ (make) every day in your country, and how many ________ (eat)?

B **Write sentences. Put the words in the correct order. Use the passive form of the verbs.**

1. chicken / often / marinate

   Chicken is often marinated.
2. eggs / often / boil

   ____
3. steak / usually / broil

   ____
4. celery / hardly ever / serve hot

   ____
5. mushrooms / often / sauté with onions

   ____
6. pasta / almost always / serve with sauce

   ____
7. muffins / always / bake in the oven

   ____
8. peanuts / usually / grow in warm places

   ____

NAME: ______________________ DATE: ______________

Grammar to Communicate 2: Simple Past: Passive

A **Complete the sentences. Circle the correct answers.**

1. The first frozen vegetables **was** / **were** sold in 1930.
2. Pasta **wasn't** / **weren't** created in Italy, but ice cream **was** / **were** invented there in the 17th century.
3. Tomatoes **was** / **were** brought to Europe in the 1700s. Many foods **wasn't** / **weren't** known in Europe until they **was** / **were** discovered by explorers like Marco Polo.
4. Rice **was** / **were** first cultivated in China thousands of years ago.
5. Do you know when potato chips **was** / **were** invented? Can you guess how many bags of chips **was** / **were** sold last year?
6. The first frozen dinner **was** / **were** sold in 1954 by a company named Swanson's.

B **Rewrite the sentences. Use the passive with *by* when necessary.**

1. People first cultivated broccoli in Italy.
   Broccoli was first cultivated in Italy.
2. The Moors introduced spinach to Europe thousands of years ago.
   ____
3. Native Americans taught the early European settlers how to grow corn.
   ____
4. In the 1500s, explorers brought new foods from the Americas to Europe.
   ____
5. They first grew tomatoes in South America.
   ____
6. People in England didn't eat tomatoes until the 1700s.
   ____

NAME: ______________________________ DATE: ______________

Grammar to Communicate 3: Passive and Active

Complete the sentences. Circle the correct answers.

1. Stir-fried vegetables **eat** / **are eaten** in many different countries.
2. The vegetables **cut up** / **are cut up**.
3. People often **stir-fry** / **are stir-fried** vegetables in a special pan.
4. This is a deep frying pan that we **call** / **are called** a wok.
5. Only a little oil **uses** / **is used** in stir-fried vegetables.
6. People usually **don't cook** / **aren't cooked** the vegetables for very long.

B **Complete the paragraph. Use the active or passive form of the verbs. Use the present or past.**

Over the years, specialty coffee houses have become very popular. The largest coffee house company in the world ___is called___ (1. call) Starbucks. The first Starbucks ____________ (2. open) in Seattle, Washington, in 1971 by three partners: two teachers and a writer. At first, the company ____________ (3. sell) only coffee beans. Businessman Howard Schultz ____________ (4. join) the company in 1982, and after a trip to Italy suggested that the company sell coffee drinks, too. This idea ____________ (5. not / like) by the owners, so Schultz ____________ (6. start) his own coffee bar chain, Il Giornale, in 1985. Two years later, Schultz ____________ (7. buy) Starbucks. Starbucks ____________ (8. begin) with 17 stores and has grown to over 6,400 coffee houses around the world. Today, these coffee houses ____________ (9. offer) more than coffee. Pastries, sandwiches, and salads ____________ (10. sell) at most Starbucks, too.

NAME: ______________________________ DATE: ______________

Review and Challenge

Find and correct the mistake in each item.

1. Many people ~~are~~ put honey and lemon in their tea.
2. A warm climate is need to grow pineapples.
3. Many kinds of fruit is cultivated in Hawaii.
4. How many hamburgers are sell in the U.S. every day?
5. Some kinds of meat are not eaten from most people in my country.
6. Don't eat that apple until it's washing.
7. Before refrigeration, people are used salt to keep food fresh.
8. A lot of olive oil are exported by Spain and Italy.
9. Many kinds of foods are brought to Asia from the New World in the 1500s.
10. Corn was eaten by people in Mexico thousands of years ago.

NAME: ______________________________ DATE: ______________

UNIT 7 VOCABULARY EXERCISE

Read the reports. Then complete the sentences. Use the words in the boxes.

Good morning, commuters. This is "Sky News Over the City," reporting a major accident on Highway 6. A car is on fire at the corner of 6 and Elmwood. We see the fire trucks arriving now. The fire is close to the houses in the area, so police are asking residents to leave. So far, no one has needed help getting out of their homes. No cars are allowed on Highway 6. Police have placed signs to direct traffic away from the intersection. If you can, find another way to get to work. Fire trucks will be blocking this area all morning.

are evacuating	clear	have posted	~~rescue~~

1. The fire department hasn't had to ___rescue___ anyone yet.
2. Police ____________________ the area.
3. Police ____________________ signs to direct traffic away from the fire.
4. The intersection is blocked now. The police will try to ____________________ the street as soon as possible.

Police are looking for a missing dog tonight, but it's not just a family pet. Daisy is a seeing-eye dog. Her owner, Katrin Olefsky, reported the dog missing from her yard at about three o'clock this afternoon when Daisy didn't come when she was called. Olefsky thinks that someone took Daisy from the yard. Police are looking carefully at the fence. They think someone cut a hole in the fence and took the dog. Seeing-eye dogs are expensive, and it will be difficult for Olefsky to get another one.

are inspecting	are searching	disappeared	replace

5. Police ____________________ for a missing dog.
6. Daisy ____________________ around three o'clock.
7. Police ____________________ the fence around the backyard.
8. The owner cannot ____________________ her seeing-eye dog because the animals are expensive.

NAME: ______________________ DATE: ____________

UNIT 7 GRAMMAR EXERCISES

Grammar to Communicate 1: Present Perfect Passive

A **Complete the sentences. Use the present perfect passive.**

1. Bicycle helmets *have been required* (require) in many U.S. cities since the mid-1990s.
2. Seat belts ____________ (install) in most cars since the late 1960s.
3. A young boy ____________ (hit) by a car and is badly injured.
4. His parents ____________ (tell), and an ambulance ____________ (call).
5. A small earthquake ____________ (report) in the Philippines.
6. The Aurora Bridge ____________ (close), and repairs ____________ (start).

B **Rewrite the sentences in the passive. If the passive can't be used, write ——.**

1. Someone has evacuated the residents.

   The residents have been evacuated.
2. The fire has forced more than 300 people to leave their homes.

   ____
3. Three firefighters have died.

   ____
4. Someone has rescued several elderly people.

   ____
5. Someone has taken more than fifty people to the hospital.

   ____
6. Someone has called the neighborhood a disaster area.

   ____

NAME: ______________________ DATE: ____________

Grammar to Communicate 2: Passive with *Need(s) to*

Complete the sentences. Use the passive with *need(s) to*. Make the sentences negative where necessary.

1. There has been an accident, and two people are badly hurt. An ambulance
   ___needs to be called___ (call).
2. A hurricane is coming. The windows ______________ (cover), and the yard furniture ______________ (bring) inside.
3. How will people know the bridge is closed? A sign
   ______________ (post).
4. A thunderstorm is coming. The beach ______________ (evacuate) right away.
5. The elevator is working fine now. The repair company
   ______________ (call).
6. We had a fire drill last week. Another one ______________ (hold) until next month.
7. The batteries in our smoke detector are really old. They
   ______________ (change) as soon as possible.
8. The fire department says that all the fire extinguishers in the building
   ______________ (inspect) every six months.
9. Most hospital visitors ______________ (tell) to speak softly when they're in the hallway. They already know they shouldn't disturb the patients.
10. The people in that plane crash ______________ (rescue) before it gets dark.
11. The bridge was badly damaged during the storm. It
    really ______________ (repair). Or maybe it
    ______________ (replace) completely.
12. This is a safe neighborhood. Your car doors ______________ (lock).
    But close the windows because it's going to rain tonight.

NAME: ______________________________ DATE: ______________

Grammar to Communicate 3: Present Progressive Passive

A **Rewrite the sentences. Use the passive. Don't use an agent.**

1. The state is building a new bridge.

   A new bridge is being built.

2. The city is cleaning up Central Park.

   ____

3. The public schools are serving healthier food for lunch.

   ____

4. The schools are also teaching students how to eat better.

   ____

5. The hospitals are holding classes for new parents.

   ____

6. The city is hiring high school students to post signs.

   ____

B **Complete the paragraph. Use the present progressive. Use the passive or active.**

Our children go back to school next week, so the city is working (1. work) hard to get ready. The buildings ______________ (2. check) to be sure they are safe and ready to go. Electrical outlets ______________ (3. inspect). Playgrounds and fields ______________ (4. clean). Batteries in smoke detectors ______________ (5. replace). Broken windows ______________ (6. fix). Fire extinguishers ______________ (7. install) on every floor, and the fire department ______________ (8. organize) a community project to teach children what to do if there is a fire at home or at school.

NAME: ______________________________ DATE: ______________

Review and Challenge

Find and correct the mistakes in the conversation. There are eight mistakes. The first one has been corrected for you.

A: I think the sprinkler system needs to ~~check~~ be checked. No one has been looked at it for a long time.

B: That's true. It need to be checked at least once a year. I'll call the company today.

A: Thanks. And what about the smoke detectors? Has the batteries been replaced recently?

B: Not really. The building is being cleaned this week. I'll ask the janitor to replace the batteries in all the smoke alarms.

A: And what about the lights in the stairs? Do some of those light bulbs need to replace, too?

B: No. After the accident, we are removed all the old bulbs and put in new ones.

A: Accident? What accident? What was happened?

B: A man fell because the light between the first and second floors was out. The light bulb needed to be replaced, but we didn't know about it until it was too late.

A: That's terrible. Well, the building is been inspected next Monday. Let's take care of all these safety things.

NAME: ______________________ DATE: ______________

UNIT 8 VOCABULARY EXERCISE

Complete the sentences. Use the words in the box.

advertisements	annoyed	commercials	exhausted	satisfying
amazed	channel	~~embarrassed~~	refreshing	

1. Jane met her new co-worker, but the next day she couldn't remember his name. She had to ask him again. Jane felt ___embarrassed___.
2. Khalil worked out at the gym for two hours. When he got home, he took a nap because he felt ______________.
3. Brian's co-worker took a two-hour lunch. Brian had to answer the phones and work alone. Brian felt ______________.
4. Most people find that a good night's sleep is ______________.
5. Omar didn't expect to get the job, but he did! He was ______________.
6. I don't think that most packaged foods are very ______________. After one of those frozen meals, I usually still feel hungry.
7. There are more ______________ in this magazine than there are articles. I'm not going to buy it anymore.
8. Benji found the program really boring, so he changed the ______________.
9. That young actor started his career by making ______________ advertising a popular computer; he was a familiar face to anyone who watched TV.

NAME: ______________________ DATE: ______________

UNIT 8 GRAMMAR EXERCISES

Grammar to Communicate 1: Adjectives Ending in *–ing* and *-ed*

A **Complete the sentences. Circle the correct answers.**

1. Try SkinSoft. We promise you won't be **disappointed / disappointing**. Millions of **satisfied / satisfying** customers can't be wrong!
2. Thirsty? Drink a Snapper, the **refreshed / refreshing** diet soda, and feel completely **energized / energizing**.
3. When your life is **exhausted / exhausting** and you feel **tired / tiring** all the time, take VitaPure. You'll be **amazed / amazing** at the difference our vitamins can make.
4. Are you looking for a magazine that doesn't have an **annoyed / annoying** advertisement on every page? Pick up a copy of our **excited / exciting** new magazine for all the **excited / exciting** news about your favorite celebrities.

B **Complete the sentences. Change the underlined verbs to adjectives with *-ing* and *-ed*.**

1. This game doesn't interest me.
   I'm not ___interested___ in this game.
   This game isn't ___interesting___.
2. Many companies say their products will amaze you.
   The products aren't really ______________.
   You won't really be ______________.
3. Most TV commercials bore me.
   I usually feel ______________ when a commercial comes on.
   I find most commercials ______________.
4. Frozen dinners don't satisfy me.
   Frozen dinners aren't ______________.
   I don't feel ______________ after eating a frozen dinner.

NAME: ______________________ DATE: ______________

Grammar to Communicate 2: *So* and *Such*

A **Complete the sentences. Use *so* or *such*.**

1. Commercials from other countries are always ___so___ interesting.
2. This is __________ a funny commercial, isn't it?
3. The actors in some ads are __________ good that you forget they're ads.
4. This shampoo will get your hair __________ clean that it will shine.
5. It was __________ a great idea to use that model in that commercial.
6. Some of the TV commercials for medicines are __________ frightening.
7. They made __________ a bad ad that no TV stations wanted to show it.
8. I don't know why commercials have to be __________ long.

B **Combine the sentences. Use *so . . . that* in 1–4. Use *such . . . that* in 5–7.**

1. The cat in that ad is so cute. I'm thinking of getting a kitten.

   The cat in that ad is so cute that I'm thinking of getting a kitten.
2. The potato chips in the ad looked good. I went out and bought some.

   ____
3. That brand of jeans is nice. I've decided to buy a pair next week.

   ____
4. The car in the commercial is fast. It looks like it's flying.

   ____
5. It was a long commercial. The company had to shorten it by 30 seconds.

   ____
6. It looks like a great restaurant. We're eating there on Saturday night.

   ____
7. It's a sad commercial. It made me cry.

   ____

NAME: ______________________ DATE: ______________

Grammar to Communicate 3: Adjective Word Order

A **Complete the sentences. Put the adjectives in the correct order.**

1. I saw an ad for a beautiful black leather handbag. (leather / beautiful / black)
2. When I saw the commercial for that ______________ car, I knew I had to have one. (sports / Japanese / small)
3. I got an ad in my mailbox today for that ______________ restaurant on Main Street. (little / French / cute)
4. After looking at hundreds of ads in bridal magazines, she finally chose a ______________ gown. (beautiful / wedding / white)
5. The director of that commercial asked for ______________ models. (young / tall / pretty)
6. I wonder why they used such ______________ furniture in that commercial. (old / ugly / wood)
7. I saw a commercial for a ______________ resort in San Juan, and I made a reservation right away. (lovely / beach / new)

B **Rewrite the sentences. Use the adjectives in parentheses.**

1. We saw an interesting commercial last night.

   We saw an interesting new commercial last night.
   (new)
2. The model in the commercial had long brown hair.

   ____
   (straight)
3. The flower shop uses red roses.

   ____
   (beautiful)
4. How many commercials has that handsome actor made?

   ____
   (young)
5. That wonderful department store is huge.

   ____
   (Spanish)

NAME: ______________________________ DATE: ______________

Review and Challenge

Find and correct the mistake in each item.

1. This is ~~so~~ such a good book that I might finish it tonight.
2. That movie was so bored that I almost fell asleep twice.
3. The actor's voice was such annoying that I turned off the TV and went to bed.
4. Studying for exams is really exhausted.
5. That cake looks so delicious than I have to have a piece.
6. You have so beautiful children.
7. My black new boots are so comfortable that I want to wear them every day.
8. My new electric pencil sharpener is so a convenient tool.
9. Some ads are so bad that they're embarrassed.
10. These picnic plastic plates were really cheap.

NAME: ______________________________ DATE: ______________

UNIT 9 VOCABULARY EXERCISE

Complete the sentences. Use the words in the box.

~~appliances~~	electricity	gadgets	toolbox	useless
assemble	engine	instruction manual	tools	

1. Don't pay too much for your next refrigerator, dishwasher, or washing machine. Come to Bargain Buys for all of your home ____appliances____.

2. There was no __________________ in the box with the bookshelves. I have no idea how to put this unit together.

3. Ellen's new laptop can run on a battery or on __________________.

4. Bryan's new bicycle came in a box with more than 20 loose pieces. It took his father over four hours to __________________ it.

5. I bought Mona a pair of special scissors that cut pizza. She loves all kinds of kitchen __________________.

6. Henry bought a used car. It needed some work, but the __________________ was still good.

7. You must have special __________________ to fix a bicycle.

8. Our ice cream maker is missing a part, and the manufacturer doesn't make the part anymore. The machine is __________________.

9. Carpenters usually keep everything they need for work in a metal __________________.

NAME: ______________________ DATE: ____________

UNIT 9 GRAMMAR EXERCISES

Grammar to Communicate 1: Adjective Clauses

A **Complete the sentences. Use *who* or *that* and the words in parentheses to write adjective clauses.**

1. An appliance that cooks food very slowly (cook food very slowly) is called a crock pot.
2. A small appliance ______________ (toast bread) is called a toaster.
3. Small devices used in the eyes ______________ (help people see) are called contact lenses.
4. A person ______________ (understand cars) is called a mechanic.
5. A small machine ______________ (curl your hair) is called a curling iron.
6. A person ______________ (fix appliances) is called an electrician.
7. A device ______________ (open bottles) is called a bottle opener.

B **Combine the sentences. Change the second sentence to an adjective clause.**

1. The people love gadgets. The people live next door to me.

   The people who live next door to me love gadgets.
2. The company is called StaySafe. The company installs the best alarm systems.

   ____
3. People buy all the newest kitchen gadgets. People love to cook.

   ____
4. The neighbors often lent me their tools. The neighbors moved.

   ____
5. The lawn mower belongs to our old neighbors. The lawn mower is in our garage.

   ____
6. The hammer also belongs to them. The hammer is in my toolbox.

   ____

NAME: ______________________ DATE: ____________

Grammar to Communicate 2: Subject and Object Relative Pronouns

A **Rewrite the sentences. Use the words in parentheses.**

1. I like to buy gifts people will find useful.

   I like to buy gifts that people will find useful.
   (that)

2. Many people buy things they don't really need.

   ____
   (which)

3. She is the person I call when I need advice.

   ____
   (who)

4. They're the friends I've known the longest.

   ____
   (that)

5. I want those lights you turn on and off by clapping your hands.

   ____
   (that)

6. I want a toolbox I can carry easily.

   ____
   (which)

B **Some of these sentences have mistakes. Find the mistakes and correct them.**

1. The vacuum cleaner I use is very quiet.
2. I bought a phone is also a camera.
3. My friend got a new laptop can burn CDs.
4. The tea I bought at the health food store is helping me lose weight.
5. My boyfriend has a clock that can tell the temperature.
6. The coffeemaker which we got as a gift makes delicious coffee.
7. This is a device makes my life much easier.
8. Do you know anyone can fix my computer?

NAME: ______________________ DATE: ______________

Grammar to Communicate 3: Relative Pronouns as Objects of Prepositions

A **Rewrite the sentences. Use relative pronouns.**

1. The store I went to was very expensive.
   The store that I went to was very expensive.
2. I couldn't afford any of the appliances I looked at.
   ____
3. The salesperson I talked to was not helpful.
   ____
4. I was disappointed by the products I saw.
   ____
5. This is the store my neighbor told me about.
   ____
6. It's a place he had heard about from his boss.
   ____
7. This neighbor is someone I may never speak to again.
   ____

B **Combine the sentences. Use *that, which,* or *who* only where necessary.**

1. This is the wonderful gadget. You've been hearing so much about it.
   This is the wonderful gadget you've been hearing so much about.
2. Who is the salesperson? You were talking to this person.
   ____
3. Which is the dishwasher? You were looking at this dishwasher.
   ____
4. Did you see the great flashlight? I told you about this flashlight.
   ____
5. Is this the device? You were looking for this device.
   ____

NAME: ______________________________ DATE: ______________

Review and Challenge

Find and correct the mistake in each item.

1. I'm looking for a gadget ~~who~~ that / which will help me open jars and bottles.
2. The people live next door to us have a garage full of strange gadgets.
3. Do you know anyone which can fix my dishwasher?
4. I got my refrigerator at the appliance store that it just opened on Main Street.
5. We have all the appliances we need them.
6. Were you satisfied with the salesperson you spoke to him?
7. Why did you buy something you didn't need it?
8. There are a lot of people which love gadgets, but I'm not one of them.
9. I saw an ad for a pen that write in ten different colors.
10. The store at the mall has the best prices is probably Gears Department Store.

NAME: ______________________________ DATE: ______________

UNIT 10 VOCABULARY EXERCISES

A **Complete the conversations. Use the words in the box.**

exchange	~~is sold out~~	refund
fitting room	rain check	try on

Salesperson: I'm sorry, but the digital camera you want ___is sold out___ (1.). I sold the last one this morning. Would you like to see a different camera?

Jack: No. I want that camera because it's on sale.

Salesperson: If you can wait, we're getting more next month. I can give you a ______________ (2.) for that camera, and you can get the sale price when the cameras arrive.

Jack: Yes. That's fine.

Salesperson: Do you want to ______________ (3.) that dress?

Noriko: Yes. I think it's my size, but I'm not sure. Where is the ______________ (4.)?

Salesperson: It's over there. If the dress doesn't fit, I'll get you a different size.

Noriko: Thanks.

Frank: I don't like this video camera. I want to return it.

Salesperson: Do you want to ______________ (5.) it for another video camera in the store?

Frank: No. I'd like a ______________ (6.), please.

Salesperson: No problem. Here's your money back.

B **Complete the conversations. Use the words in the box.**

find out	has been in business	restroom	wonder

Maria: I ______________________ (1.) if I can return this sweater if George doesn't like it.

Beatriz: I think you can, but let's ______________________ (2.) for sure. Just ask the cashier.

Vince: Wow, this car is really beautiful!

Salesperson: Would you like to take it for a drive?

Vince: Oh, there's no way I can buy this car! It's much too expensive.

Salesperson: Well, come into my office and we can talk about it. I'm sure I can find a great car for you. This company ______________________ (3.) for over twenty years.

Vince: No, really. I can't buy it. My car is still good. I was just looking for a men's room.

Salesperson: Oh. Well, the ______________________ (4.) is inside and to the right.

Vince: Thanks.

NAME: ______________________________ DATE: ______________

UNIT 10 GRAMMAR EXERCISES

Grammar to Communicate I: Noun Clauses: Question Words and *That*

Underline the noun clauses.

1. I don't think the store opens until 10:00 A.M.
2. I don't know when the next bus will be here.
3. I'm afraid that we are all sold out of that item.
4. I'm glad you checked the size before you bought it.
5. I'm sorry that shirt didn't fit you.
6. I'm not sure where the post office is.
7. I wonder when the sale ends.

B **Complete each sentence. Circle the correct letter of the correct answer.**

1. I can see ______ you love your new shirt. It's really nice.

   (a.) why   b. where   c. that   d. what

2. I hope ______ you will be happy with your purchase.

   a. when   b. that   c. what   d. where

3. I'd like to know ______ the restrooms are.

   a. where   b. who   c. that   d. why

4. I'm happy ______ you found such a nice gift for your mother.

   a. when   b. who   c. why   d. that

5. I'd like to know ______ he doesn't like this store.

   a. that   b. who   c. why   d. where

6. I'm not sure ______ this store closes.

   a. who   b. where   c. what   d. when

7. I wonder ______ all the sales associates are.

   a. where   b. what   c. that   d. why

NAME: ______________________________ DATE: ______________

Grammar to Communicate 2: Noun Clauses: Indirect Questions

A **Write questions. Put the words in the correct order.**

1. do / where / know / I / good / you / a / shoe store / find / can

   Do you know where I can find a good shoe store?

2. me / got / where / you / tell / jeans / can / you / your

   ____

3. closes / you / do / what time / the / know / store

   ____

4. could / me / how much / costs / this sweater / tell / you

   ____

5. remember / what size / do / you / wears / he

   ____

B **Complete the conversations. Read the answers. Then complete the questions.**

1. **A:** Do you know how long this store has been in business?

   B: Believe it or not, this store has been in business for almost 50 years.

2. **A:** Can you tell me ______________________________

   B: These gloves are $39.00.

3. **A:** Could you tell me ______________________________

   B: You can find a restroom on the third floor and on the eighth floor.

4. **A:** Do you know ______________________________

   B: The restroom is closed because it's being cleaned.

5. **A:** Could you please tell me ______________________________

   B: It's a quarter to two.

NAME: ______________________ DATE: ______________

Grammar to Communicate 3: Noun Clauses: *If / Whether*

A **Complete the conversations.**

1. **A:** Can you give me a refund without a receipt?
   B: Let me ask the manager if I can give you a refund without a receipt.
2. **A:** I wonder if the store will allow me to return shoes.
   B: I don't know whether ______________________.
3. **A:** Do you have this sweatshirt in a large?
   B: I'll check to see if ______________________.
4. **A:** Did they give you a receipt for those pants?
   B: I don't know if ______________________.
5. **A:** Do I have time to try on this shirt before the store closes?
   B: I'm not sure whether ______________________.
6. **A:** Did the store have that skirt in other colors?
   B: I don't remember if ______________________.

B **Write questions or statements. Put the words in the correct order.**

1. you / whether / do / jewelry / sells / this store / know / ?
   Do you know whether this store sells jewelry?
2. can't remember / or / I / paid / whether / with cash / I / with a credit card / .
   ____
3. you / there's / nearby / know / payphone / if / a / do / ?
   ____
4. I / if / comfortable / shoes / will be / don't know / these / very / .
   ____
5. whether / match / not sure / this / skirt / I'm / color / will / my / .
   ____

NAME: ______________________ DATE: ____________

Review and Challenge

Find the mistake in each item. Circle the letter and correct the mistake.

1. I don't know what size is it.
   A B C (D)

   Correct: it is

2. Do you know where is the cosmetic department?
   A B C D

   Correct: ______________________

3. She couldn't remember where she did buy her scarf.
   A B C D

   Correct: ______________________

4. Can you remember whether you did get a receipt?
   A B C D

   Correct: ______________________

5. Do you know if the store does sell film?
   A B C D

   Correct: ______________________

6. I don't know that if the store gives rain checks.
   A B C D

   Correct: ______________________

7. Could you tell me how much do these sunglasses cost?
   A B C D

   Correct: ______________________

8. I'm wondering if you do have a catalogue I could take with me.
   A B C D

   Correct: ______________________

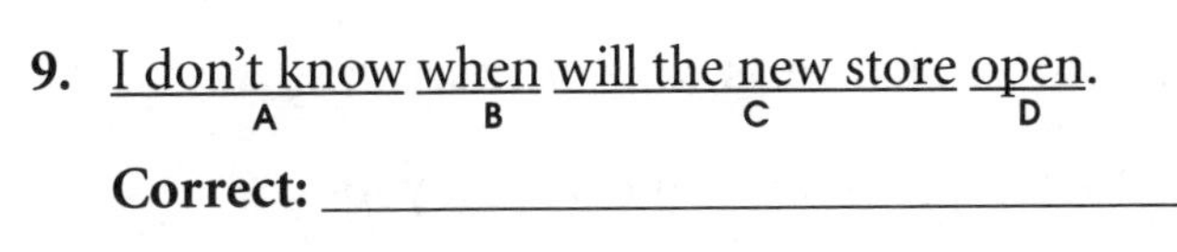

9. I don't know when will the new store open.
   A B C D

   Correct: ______________________

10. I wonder if these jeans will look good on me?
    A B C D

    Correct: ______________________

NAME: ______________________________ DATE: ______________

UNIT 11 VOCABULARY EXERCISES

A **Complete the paragraph. Use the words in the box.**

~~accepted~~	dormitory	financial aid	live on campus	move in

In April, Tarek got good news. California State ___accepted___ (1.) him to the university. In addition, he received enough ______________ (2.) to pay for his classes and books. He has to pay for his housing, so now he is looking for an inexpensive place to live. He prefers to ______________ (3.) because he doesn't want to drive to classes in the morning, but there aren't many choices for housing. There is a ______________ (4.), but Tarek isn't sure he wants to live there. It may be noisy, and he may not be able to sleep well. Tarek is also looking at some apartments close to campus. He hopes to ______________ (5.) by August 15th.

B **Complete the conversation. Use the words in the box.**

give my notice	salary requirements

Mr. Adams: You're a great manager, Lillian. If you're ever looking for a job, I have a position for you at Adams Accounting.

Lillian: I've been thinking about a career change. Is your offer serious?

Mr. Adams: Very serious. You can start working for me tomorrow, if you want.

Lillian: I have to ______________ (1.) to my current employer, but I like the idea of working for Adams Accounting.

Mr. Adams: Let's talk about this some more. Let me know your ______________ (2.). I'm pretty sure I can pay you more than what you earn now.

NAME: ______________________ DATE: ______________

UNIT 11 GRAMMAR EXERCISES

Grammar to Communicate 1: Reported Speech: Statements

A **Complete the sentences. Change the quoted speech to reported speech.**

1. Maria said, "I want to find a new roommate."

   Maria said that she wanted to find a new roommate.

2. John said, "I've already done my homework."

   John said ______________________

3. Ava said, "Sam can help Yolanda write her résumé."

   Ava said that ______________________

4. Tom said, "I'm too tired to go to class today."

   Tom said that ______________________

5. The girls said, "We're looking for a two-bedroom apartment."

   The girls said ______________________

6. Dora said, "I love living on campus."

   Dora said that ______________________

7. Michelle said, "I'll try to live on campus next year."

   Michelle said ______________________

B **Complete the sentences. Use *said* or *told*.**

1. The applicant ___told___ the interviewer his salary requirements.
2. Hiromi __________ she planned to apply for financial aid.
3. Harry __________ he had been accepted to the state university
4. She __________ her roommate to turn the music down.
5. They __________ me they were going to move in soon.
6. He __________ he was going to the library after class.

NAME: ______________________ DATE: ______________

Grammar to Communicate 2: Reported Speech: Information Questions

A **Rewrite the sentences as reported speech. Begin each sentence with *The interviewer asked me*.**

1. "How long did you work at your last job?"

   The interviewer asked me how long I had worked at my last job.

2. "What skills do you have?"

   ____

3. "How did you hear about the job?"

   ____

4. "When did you finish high school?"

   ____

5. "Why don't you have a résumé?"

   ____

B **Write the exact words that the speakers used. Use quotation marks.**

1. The interviewer asked what my salary requirements were.

   "What are your salary requirements?"

2. The interviewer asked me where I had gone to college.

   ____

3. The interviewer wanted to know why I had left my last job.

   ____

4. The interviewer asked how far away I lived from the office.

   ____

5. The interviewer wondered when I could start the job.

   ____

NAME: ______________________ DATE: ______________

Grammar to Communicate 3: Reported Speech: *Yes / No* Questions

A **Match the quotes with the reported *yes / no* questions. Write the correct letters. Use one of the reported questions twice.**

_a_ **1.** "Were you on time?"	**a.** He asked whether I had been on time.
____ **2.** "Are you on time?"	**b.** He asked if I would be on time.
____ **3.** "Have you been on time?"	**c.** He asked if I was on time.
____ **4.** "Will you be on time?"	

B **Read the questions. Then complete the sentences. Use reported speech.**

1. "Are your instructors helpful?"

   She asked _if my instructors were helpful_.

2. "Is the campus bus usually on time?"

   He asked ______________________.

3. "Have many students been given financial aid this year?"

   She asked ______________________.

4. "Are you taking more than three classes?"

   My professor asked ______________________.

5. "Did you find a roommate?"

   My friend asked me ______________________.

6. "Are you going to get a part-time job?"

   My parents asked ______________________.

7. "Will you be in class today?"

   Another student asked me ______________________.

NAME: ______________________________ DATE: ______________

Review and Challenge

Find and correct the mistake in each item.

1. George said that he really ~~wants~~ wanted to get a new laptop.
2. Emma told me her interview yesterday went very well.
3. Marla asked me if I am interested in studying with her tonight.
4. Regis said that the program will accept more international students.
5. Jack told the interviewer he was at his old job for two years.
6. Crystal said she is sorry for making so much noise last night.
7. The teacher said us there would be a test on Friday.
8. Audrey told she was going to live off campus next year.
9. He asked whether I can start the job on April 1st.
10. I asked the cashier how late did the bookstore stayed open.

NAME: ______________________________ DATE: ______________

UNIT 12 VOCABULARY EXERCISE

Complete the paragraphs. Use the words in the boxes.

has trouble	postpones	succeed in	~~takes pride in~~	wastes time

Ed and Yu are roommates. Unfortunately, they are very different. Ed is very messy. Yu is very neat. Yu takes pride in (1.) a clean house. That's why he washes the dishes, vacuums the floor, and puts his clothes away. Ed doesn't care about having a clean house. He leaves his shoes on the sofa and never washes a dish. Yu reminds him to clean, but Ed ____________ (2.) remembering to do his chores. Ed says he's busy with school or worried about exams, but Yu thinks Ed ____________ (3.) his chores because he's lazy. In fact, Ed often ____________ (4.) reading comic books and playing computer games. Yu has decided that if he doesn't ____________ (5.) making Ed into a better roommate soon, he'll have to find someone else to live with.

be capable of	be curious	can't help	socializes

Some people are good at sales. Why is that? A good salesperson usually has "social intelligence." He or she likes to meet other people and ____________ (6.) easily at parties and meetings. A good salesperson should ____________ (7.) making conversation on many different topics. It is important to ____________ (8.) about the lives and interests of other people and really listen to their concerns. And here's one more secret: Good salespeople ____________ (9.) trying to make a sale—it makes no difference where they are! Some people think it's in their blood!

NAME: ______________________ DATE: ____________

UNIT 12 GRAMMAR EXERCISES

Grammar to Communicate 1: Gerunds as Subjects

A **Complete the sentences. Use the gerund form of the verbs in parentheses.**

1. Being popular (be popular) was important to me when I was younger.
2. ______________ (have a lot of friends) was my dream.
3. ______________ (get along with people) is easy for me.
4. ______________ (not treat others badly) is my life goal.
5. ______________ (try to be kind) is more important now.
6. ______________ (not hate anyone) is also important to me.

B **Rewrite the sentences. Begin with a gerund.**

1. It is wonderful to make friends with your classmates.

   Making friends with your classmates is wonderful.
2. It is fun to spend time with friends after class.

   ____
3. It's hard to work in pairs with people you don't know well.

   ____
4. It bothers me to work with someone I don't know.

   ____
5. It's helpful to ask each other questions about the new grammar.

   ____
6. It doesn't bother me to make grammar mistakes sometimes.

   ____

NAME: ______________________________ DATE: ______________

Grammar to Communicate 2: Gerunds as Objects of Prepositions

A **Complete the sentences. Use the correct prepositions. Use *at*, *in*, *of*, or *with*.**

1. John is very good ___at___ making people feel comfortable.
2. Lillian never gets tired __________ talking to her friends.
3. Henry takes great pride __________ hosting great dinner parties.
4. Dianne believes __________ treating others in the same way that she would like to be treated.
5. Sylvia is capable __________ doing several things at the same time.
6. Danny is interested __________ getting to know people from many different cultures.
7. Fong is bored __________ studying every night.

B **Write sentences. Use the gerund form of the verbs. Add prepositions where necessary.**

1. Gonzalo / be / better / read in English / than speak

   Gonzalo is better at reading in English than at speaking.
2. he / learn / new vocabulary / write it / in his notebook

   ____
3. Gonzalo / never succeed / finish anything / on time

   ____
4. the poor guy / be not capable / sit in one place / for a long time

   ____
5. he / get tired / work on the same thing / very quickly

   ____
6. I / take great pride / help / my friend / improve his English

   ____

NAME: ______________________ DATE: ____________

Grammar to Communicate 3: Gerunds As Objects of Verbs

A **Complete the conversations. Use the correct form of the verbs in the box.**

be	break up	do	~~go~~	make	spend

1. **A:** Why does Wanda waste her time ___going___ out with Henry?

   B: She knows he's not right for her, but she's having a hard time __________ with him.

2. **A:** You need to stop __________ things that are bad for you.

   B: I know that. I just keep __________ the wrong decisions.

3. **A:** I have trouble __________ alone. Any suggestions?

   B: Yes. You need to practice __________ time by yourself. It's not so bad, you know.

B **Complete the sentences about Halle and Tito. Use the words in parentheses.**

Halle thinks doing things alone is great. She . . .

- has a hard time ___getting along with people.___
  1. (get along with people)
- can't stand ______________________
  2. (talk on the phone)
- has stopped ______________________
  3. (go out with friends)
- avoids ______________________
  4. (meet new people)

Tito thinks doing things alone is boring. He . . .

- has trouble ______________________
  5. (not be with other people)
- can't stop ______________________
  6. (think of ways to make friends)
- enjoys ______________________
  7. (talk to strangers)
- spends a lot of time ______________________
  8. (make plans to socialize)

NAME: ______________________________ DATE: ______________

Review and Challenge

Find and correct the mistake in each sentence.

1. ~~To speak~~ Speaking to a large group of people makes Mihoko nervous.
2. In fact, she can't stand speak in public.
3. She is very good in helping people find solutions to their problems.
4. No having any friends can be very difficult for children.
5. Many children have trouble to socialize with others.
6. Play with children their own age is a real problem for many.
7. Parents need to help their children understand that learning to get along with other kids are very important.
8. Mihoko enjoys helps parents help their children.
9. Working with children are her job—and her love.
10. She spends a lot of time help kids, and she loves doing it.

NAME: ______________________ DATE: ______________

UNIT 13 VOCABULARY EXERCISE

Complete the diary entry. Use the words in the box.

convince	~~encouraged~~	managed	promised	warned
didn't mind	expected	pretended	refused	

I have always loved music. When I was a child, my parents noticed that I liked to play the piano. They encouraged (1.) me to take lessons. At first, I liked to practice. I __________ (2.) playing the same notes over and over. Music was fun. Then the music became more difficult. I became frustrated and tired. One day, I didn't want to play anymore. I __________ (3.) to practice.

My parents tried to __________ (4.) me to practice. They __________ (5.) many good things if I continued to play. For example, I didn't have to do the dishes or wash the car if I practiced. I still said I didn't want to play the piano. My parents tried again. They __________ (6.) me that I had to practice or they wouldn't allow me to watch TV. I still said I didn't want to play the piano.

After two months, my parents stopped telling me to practice. I was surprised. I never __________ (7.) them to stop. Instead, they said they were going to sell my piano. They called their friends to find a buyer, and they put an ad in the newspaper. I __________ (8.) not to care, but I felt really sad. One day, I went to the piano and started playing my favorite songs. That's how my parents finally __________ (9.) to make me practice. And no, they never sold my piano.

NAME: ______________________________ DATE: ______________

UNIT 13 GRAMMAR EXERCISES

Grammar to Communicate 1: *Used To Do* and *Be Used To Doing*

A **Complete each sentence. Circle the letter of the correct answer.**

1. I work in an office, but I __________ work at a bank.

   (a.) used to **b.** am getting used to **c.** am used to

2. Life in the country seems very boring to Gina, and she __________ living on a farm.

   a. is used to **b.** isn't used to **c.** is getting used to

3. Joshua works 11 hours a day at his new job, but that's OK because he __________ working long hours.

   a. didn't use to **b.** is used to **c.** used to

4. Waking up at 5:00 A.M. is a little hard for me, but I __________ it.

   a. used to **b.** was used to **c.** am getting used to

5. When I was a child, I __________ ride my bicycle to school every day.

   a. used to **b.** was used to **c.** got used to

6. I didn't __________ like broccoli, but now I love it!

   a. used to **b.** be used to **c.** use to

B **How have the people's lives changed? Complete the sentences. Use *used to* in 1–3. Use *be used to* in 4–6. Some sentences are negative.**

1. We live in an apartment now. <u>We used to live</u> in a house.
2. I have a cat. I __________ a pet, so I'm still getting used to it.
3. We take the subway now. We __________ the bus.
4. People can shop 24 hours a day here. We __________ after 10:00 P.M.
5. We had always lived in a house. We still __________ in an apartment.
6. I don't like taking care of my cat. I __________ care of a pet.

NAME: ______________________ DATE: ______________

Grammar to Communicate 2: Verb + Infinitive or Gerund

A **Look at the verbs. Are they followed by a gerund, by an infinitive, or by either one? Write *G* for *gerund*, *I* for *infinitive*, or *GI* for either *gerund* or *infinitive*.**

1.	hate	love	like	GI
2.	expect	hope	want	____
3.	promise	refuse	manage	____
4.	enjoy	don't mind	avoid	____
5.	learn	need	plan	____
6.	can't stand	try	start	____
7.	allow	pretend	offer	____

B **Complete the sentences. Write the gerund or infinitive. More than one answer may be possible.**

1. We expected to take (take) a test today, but it was delayed until tomorrow.
2. The students were warned not __________ (run) in the halls during a fire drill.
3. I promised __________ (call) my parents once a week.
4. It was such a beautiful day that I didn't mind __________ (wait) for the bus.
5. I have managed __________ (do) really well in all my classes this year.
6. Even though he was encouraged not to be shy, Benjamin couldn't stand __________ (be) called on in class.
7. Ms. Sanders pretended not __________ (know) about the surprise party the students had planned for her.
8. I convinced Ian __________ (register) in a TOEFL prep class.
9. Many students don't enjoy __________ (have to) sit all day.

NAME: ______________________________ DATE: ______________

Grammar to Communicate 3: Verb + Object + Infinitive

A **Underline the object in each sentence.**

1. The principal warned <u>the students</u> to be careful of the broken glass.
2. The teacher encouraged her class to bring raingear for their field trip.
3. I convinced Marsha to take a more challenging math class.
4. We would like you to apply to more than one college.
5. Her parents encouraged her to finish college before getting married.
6. My mother always wanted me to get my homework done early.
7. Ken's parents didn't allow him to have a job while he was in high school.

B **Rewrite the sentences. Use the verbs in parentheses.**

1. Hiro's father said, "Don't get married until you finish college."

   Hiro's father advised him not to get married until he finished college.
   (advise)
2. Maureen's best friend said, "Don't make your decision too quickly."

   ____
   (encourage)
3. Carlos's teacher said, "Correct the errors in your paper."

   ____
   (want)
4. Susana's mother said, "Learn to be independent before you get married."

   ____
   (remind)
5. Our grandparents said, "Don't move too far away."

   ____
   (ask)
6. Tom told me, "You are going to be very successful."

   ____
   (expect)

NAME: ______________________________ DATE: ______________

Review and Challenge

Find and correct the mistake in each item.

1. He hopes ~~getting~~ to get a good grade this quarter.
2. Ginny and Tom decided to not get married until next year.
3. My new job is difficult, but I'm getting use to it. Working ten hours a day isn't so hard.
4. The teacher asked he again and again to please be quiet.
5. I use to take the bus to school, but now I carpool with my friend.
6. Karl is used to stay up until midnight to study.
7. I really dislike to sit in the back of the class.
8. Patty's mother advised her not taking too many difficult classes.
9. She promised practicing the piano every day.
10. I'm used to belong to the school swim team, but I don't anymore.

NAME: ______________________________ DATE: ______________

UNIT 14 VOCABULARY EXERCISE

Match the sentences with the correct responses. Write the correct letters.

__d__ **1.** Are you going to have a big party for your 50th birthday?

____ **2.** What are you doing this Sunday morning at around 10:00?

____ **3.** Are you making a lot of food for the party?

____ **4.** I'm too tired to cook, and I don't want to go to a restaurant.

____ **5.** Oh, there's the bell! They're here.

____ **6.** Hi, John! Thanks for inviting me.

____ **7.** Do you want to cook some fish tonight?

____ **8.** Do you want to take a ride in my new car? We could go on a picnic.

a. No. I want to go out to a restaurant. I don't feel like cooking.

b. Let's have some Mexican takeout. I'll pick it up on my way home.

c. I'd love that. It's a lovely day to go for a drive.

d. Not really. I just want to have a get-together with close friends.

e. No, just a big salad. It's a potluck.

f. I'll get the door.

g. I'm having brunch with my parents.

h. I can take your coat. How about something to drink?

NAME: ______________________________ DATE: ______________

UNIT 14 GRAMMAR EXERCISES

Grammar to Communicate I: Suggestions and Offers: *Let's/Let Me/Why Don't We/Why Don't I*

A **Find the mistake in each item. Circle the letter and correct the mistake.**

1. Let's (A) to plan (B) a get-together (C) at (D) our house next weekend.
   Correct: plan

2. Why don't we (A) ask (B) Sally and Roger to meet (C) us for brunch on Sunday morning. (D)
   Correct: ____________________

3. Let's (A) no (B) cook tonight. Let's (C) order (D) take-out.
   Correct: ____________________

4. Let me (A) to get (B) the door for you (C). Your hands are full. Why don't I (D) help you?
   Correct: ____________________

5. What a beautiful day! Why (A) we don't (B) go (C) for a drive (D)?
   Correct: ____________________

6. Let's go out (A) to a restaurant (B) celebrating (C) your birthday next week. (D)
   Correct: ____________________

7. Why I don't (A) take (B) your coat? Let me (C) have (D) it.
   Correct: ____________________

B **Complete the sentences. Circle the correct word or phrase.**

1. **Let's / Let me** go for a bike ride together later this afternoon.
2. **Why not / Why don't I** help you carry the trashcans out to the street?
3. **Let's / Let's not** go to the neighbors' party. It should be fun!
4. **Let me / Why don't we** offer to help Elaine wash the dishes?
5. **Why don't we not / Let's not** eat at this restaurant again. It's horrible!
6. **Let's not / Why don't we** have a party this weekend. I'm not in the mood.
7. **Let me / Let's** pick you up from work this evening.

NAME: ______________________________ DATE: ______________

Grammar to Communicate 2: Preferences: *Would Rather / Would Prefer*

A **Complete the sentences. Use *would rather* or *would prefer*.**

1. I don't want to see a horror film. I ___would rather___ go to a comedy.
2. We ____________________ spend our free time playing tennis or swimming.
3. I ____________________ buy new furniture, but my husband ____________________ to go on a trip.
4. We'll have to ask Pedro, but I think he ____________________ to have a cookout on Sunday.
5. When we're on vacation, we ____________________ stay in small hotels. We don't like large hotels.
6. ____________________ you ____________________ to sit at a table outside, or ____________________ you ____________________ sit inside in the air conditioning?

B **Write questions. Use *Would you rather . . . or . . . ?* in 1–4. Use *Would you prefer to . . . or . . . ?* in 5–8.**

1. ___Would you rather go shopping downtown or take the bus to the mall?___
(go shopping downtown / take the bus to the mall)
2. ____
(play tennis / go swimming)
3. ____
(have a small party / invite all your friends)
4. ____
(go out to a restaurant / get take-out)
5. ____
(socialize with friends on Saturday night / stay home alone)
6. ____
(watch TV / read a good book)
7. ____
(play word games / sports)
8. ____
(spend time with new friends / old friends)

NAME: ______________________________ DATE: ______________

Grammar to Communicate 3: Polite Requests: *Would You Mind*

A **Rewrite the requests. Use *Would you mind.***

1. Please help me with the dishes.

   Would you mind helping me with the dishes?

2. Would you let me use your phone?

   ____

3. Could you please open the door for me?

   ____

4. Can you drive me to class tomorrow?

   ____

5. Please hand me that pen.

   ____

6. Could you please help me with this grammar?

   ____

B **You are a teacher. Ask different students to help you. Use *Would you mind.***

1. The board needs to be erased. Ask Andrea.

   Andrea, would you mind erasing the board?

2. The new books need to be put on the shelf. Ask Erin.

   ____

3. It's getting dark. Ask Will to turn on the lights.

   ____

4. It's getting cold. Ask Joanne to close the windows.

   ____

5. You'd like to collect the students' homework. Ask Walter.

   ____

6. Ask Bob to help you take your things to your car.

   ____

NAME: ______________________________ DATE: ______________

Review and Challenge

Find and correct the mistake in each item.

1. Jean would ~~not prefer~~ prefer not to stay out very late tonight. She has to get up early tomorrow.
2. Why don't I carrying your books for you?
3. Would you mind to take my coat?
4. We'd rather to have brunch on Saturday.
5. Would you prefer to walk to the store or to drive?
6. Would you mind giving me a ride? Yes, I'd be happy to.
7. Let's to stay home tonight.
8. Why don't we see a movie tonight.
9. Would you rather go skiing or going ice-skating?
10. Let me helps Jimmy with his homework.

NAME: ______________________ DATE: ____________

UNIT 15 VOCABULARY EXERCISES

A **Complete the sentences. Use the words in the box.**

crosswalk	left lane	~~pedestrian~~	walk signal
intersection	parallel park	right lane	

Rules of the Road

1. If you are a ___pedestrian___, look left and right before you walk across the street.
2. When you want to cross a busy street, press the button for the ______________.
3. When you cross the street, stay in the ______________.
4. In the United States, cars drive in the ______________.
5. In the United Kingdom, cars drive in the ______________.
6. When you want to park between two cars at the side of the street, you have to ______________.
7. There is usually a traffic signal at a busy ______________.

B **Look at the pictures. Then complete the sentences. Circle the letter of the correct answer.**

1. We need to __________. There's a police car behind us!

   a. pass **b.** pull over **c.** speed

2. Never __________ another car when you are going up a hill.

   a. pass **b.** pull over **c.** speed

3. Don't go too fast or too slowly. Drive at a safe __________.

   a. pass **b.** pull over **c.** speed

NAME: ______________________ DATE: ____________

UNIT 15 GRAMMAR EXERCISES

Grammar to Communicate 1: *Should / Ought to / Had better*

A **Write affirmative and negative statements or questions. Use *ought to*. If *ought to* is not possible, use *should*.**

1. You don't parallel park very well. You ought to practice more.
   (you / practice more)
2. We don't have much gas. ______________________
   (we / start looking for a gas station)
   ____
3. What's that terrible noise the car is making? ______________________
   (we / pull over)
   ____
4. You're going much too fast. ______________________
   (you / drive above 30 mph here)
5. Drive faster! ______________________
   (you / drive at least 55 mph on the highway)
6. The traffic will be awful soon. ______________________
   (what time / we / leave the house)
7. It's too hard to find parking downtown. ______________________
   (you / drive your car into the city)
   ____

B **Complete the advice. Use *had better* or *had better not*. Use contractions.**

1. There's a big traffic jam on Main Street. We 'd better take (take) another route.
2. The light is yellow. You ______________ (stop).
3. There's an ambulance coming. We ______________ (pull over).
4. Your road test is tomorrow. You ______________ (go) to bed late tonight.
5. They gave you a parking ticket. You ______________ (throw) it away.
6. This ticket needs to be paid by next week. You ______________ (mail) the check tomorrow.

NAME: ______________________________ DATE: ______________

Grammar to Communicate 2:
Have to / Be supposed to / Can

A **Complete the sentences. Use the correct form of *be (not) supposed to* + verb.**

1. Slow down! You _'re supposed to slow down_ in a school zone.
2. Oh, no! I want to make a U-Turn, but the sign says you __________________ a U-Turn here. I hope no one sees me!
3. I think I'm going to pass that truck. I know I __________________ in this section of the highway, but he's driving only 40 miles an hour.
4. Why do people use cell phones while they're driving? We all know we __________________ them, but so many of us do.
5. When a school bus stops to let children off, cars __________________ and wait for the bus to start up again.

B **Read these driving situations. Complete the sentences. Use *can't, have to, has to, doesn't have to,* or *don't have to.***

1. Yolanda sees a No U-turn sign. She _can't_ turn left or right. She __________________ keep going straight.
2. You __________________ hold the baby in your lap. It's against the law. She __________________ be in her car seat. Also, the car seat __________________ be in the back seat. It __________________ be up here with us in the front seat.
3. I guess we __________________ pass that slow car now. We __________________ wait until we're out of this No-Passing Zone.
4. Oh, no! We __________________ turn on this street. It's one way. Well, we __________________ go very far out of our way. Just one more block.
5. I'm so glad they removed the stoplight at this corner. There's a Stop sign now, so drivers __________________ stop. But they __________________ wait for ten minutes for the light to change!

NAME: ______________________________ DATE: ______________

Grammar to Communicate 3: *Had to, Was / Were supposed to*

A **Complete the sentences. Circle the correct answers.**

1. Sorry we're late! We **had to / didn't have to** stop and buy gas.
2. There were no pedestrians on the street, so we **had to / didn't have to** stop at the crosswalk.
3. We just missed the turn. We **were supposed to / weren't supposed to** turn left at the last light.
4. How many times **were you supposed to / did you have to** take the road test before you finally passed it?
5. I **was supposed to / wasn't supposed to** drive my father's sports car while he was gone. I hope he doesn't find out that I used it on Saturday night.
6. He got a ticket because he **didn't have to / wasn't supposed to** drive without a seat belt, but he did.

B **Complete the sentences. Use the correct affirmative or negative form of *had to* or *was / were supposed to*.**

1. I ___was supposed to___ take my car to the carwash this morning, but I didn't have time.
2. We ____________________ drive to the beach, but we decided to take the train at the last minute.
3. That police officer ____________________ give us a ticket. It wasn't necessary. He was just being mean.
4. I don't think you ____________________ turn. There was a red arrow.
5. Michiko ____________________ take her road test twice before she passed it.
6. My high school offered a class called Drivers' Ed. We ____________________ take it, but most of us did. We wanted to get our licenses as soon as possible.

NAME: ______________________________ DATE: ______________

Review and Challenge

Find and correct the mistake in each item.

1. Where ~~ought~~ should I take this car in for service?
2. We were supposed take our road test yesterday, but we forgot.
3. You better slow down on Main Street. The police are giving a lot of tickets.
4. We can't to turn here. We have to go to the next corner.
5. You didn't had to tell me to slow down. I saw the sign.
6. I haven't to drive at all yesterday. My wife drove the whole way.
7. You'd better no go over the speed limit downtown. There are cameras at almost all the lights.
8. I'm supposed to study for my road test last night, but I had no time. I'll do it tonight.
9. We had to pay almost $100 for two parking tickets. The city should has more parking garages.
10. We ought not pull over here. This is a dangerous intersection.

NAME: ______________________ DATE: ______________

UNIT 16 VOCABULARY EXERCISE

Complete the article. Use the words in the box.

blow away	destroyed	flood	loses power	stock up on
board up	flashlight	~~hurricanes~~	predict	

Hurricanes (1.) are terrible storms with high wind and a lot of rain. Scientists can usually ______ (2.) when a hurricane is coming, but they don't know exactly where it will go. If you find out that a hurricane is coming to your area, ______ (3.) canned food and bottled water. Buy a ______ (4.) in case the electricity goes out. That way, if your house ______ (5.), you'll be able to see in the dark. If you have large windows in your house or business, ______ (6.) the windows with wood. Covering the windows can prevent damage. Also, bring everything inside. During a hurricane, the strong winds can ______ (7.) trash cans and yard furniture.

Sometimes you can't totally prepare for a hurricane. If there is a lot of rain, the streets will ______ (8.) and water will come in. Many homes and businesses can be ______ (9.) in a hurricane. And many lives can be lost.

NAME: ______________________ DATE: ______________

UNIT 16 GRAMMAR EXERCISES

Grammar to Communicate 1: *Should have* for Regrets about the Past

A **Complete the sentences with *should have* and the verbs in parentheses. Add *not* where necessary.**

1. You should have boarded up (board up) the windows before the hurricane hit.
2. We ______________ (buy) batteries for our flashlights.
3. We ______________ (wait) so long before we went to the supermarket. There wasn't much food left in the store.
4. We ______________ (take) the warnings more seriously.
5. You ______________ (get) more water. Now we only have one gallon left.
6. We ______________ (waste) our money on ice cream.

B **Imagine that there was a hurricane in your area. Your neighbors didn't pay attention to the warnings and made a lot of mistakes. Write sentences with *should have*. Write negative sentences where necessary.**

1. They didn't stock up on drinking water and canned foods.

   They should have stocked up on drinking water and canned foods.

2. They went to the beach on the morning of the storm.

   ____

3. They didn't check that they had a flashlight and batteries.

   ____

4. They didn't buy candles.

   ____

5. They ignored all the warnings.

   ____

6. They didn't believe the forecasters.

   ____

NAME: ______________________ DATE: ______________

Grammar to Communicate 2: *May have / Might have* for Past Possibility

A **Imagine that it's the day after a terrible storm. Complete the conversations. Use *may have* or *might have* and the verbs in parentheses.**

1. A: The Carsons' car isn't in their driveway.

   B: They <u>might / may have put</u> (put) it in the garage.

2. A: I wonder why the Sotos didn't evacuate.

   B: They ______________ (not / have) time.

3. A: Where do you think the Harrisons went?

   B: They ______________ (go) to stay with Mrs. Harrison's family.

4. A: Did you notice that the Tanakas' lights are on?

   B: They ______________ (leave) them on for a good reason.

5. A: The Lees' dog is in the front yard.

   B: They ______________ (forget) to take him inside.

B **Rewrite the sentences. Use *may have* in 1–3 and *might have* in 4–6.**

1. Maybe the neighbors didn't know the storm was coming.

   <u>The neighbors may not have known the storm was coming.</u>

2. Perhaps they didn't listen to the weather forecast.

   ____

3. Maybe they were out all day.

   ____

4. Perhaps they came home earlier in the day.

   ____

5. Maybe they decided to drive to the city.

   ____

6. Perhaps they made the wrong decision.

   ____

NAME: ______________________________ DATE: ______________

Grammar to Communicate 3: *Must have* for Logical Conclusions about the Past

A **Complete the sentences with *must have* and the verbs. Use the passive where necessary.**

1. I didn't feel the earthquake, so it _must not have been_ (not / be) very strong.
2. You ____________ (be) very busy at the time, because the earthquake was quite strong.
3. All the animals in the zoo started acting strangely before the earthquake. They ____________ (feel) something.
4. After the earthquake, parts of the city were dark. The power ____________ (go) out.
5. The people who lost power didn't know what was happening. They ____________ (call) 911.
6. A lot of people were injured downtown. Ambulances ____________ (send) from all the local hospitals.

B **Rewrite the sentences. Use *must have*.**

1. You probably felt terrified during the earthquake.
   You must have felt terrified during the earthquake.
2. People probably didn't think they were going to survive.
   ____
3. The emergency phone lines were probably busy all night.
   ____
4. Many people were probably taken to the hospital.
   ____
5. The fire department probably had to use all their trucks.
   ____
6. The city was probably a very frightening place.
   ____

NAME: ______________________________ DATE: ____________

Review and Challenge

Find and correct the mistake in each item.

1. We should ~~called~~ *have called* the insurance company after the storm, but we didn't.
2. Oh, look. The clock has the wrong time. The power must to have gone out while we were out.
3. Mark's car isn't in the driveway. He may have went to stay with his parents for a few days.
4. There's no smoke coming from the building, and the firefighters have left. The fire might have been put out.
5. The earthquake registered 7.5 on the Richter scale. It must has been terrifying!
6. I'm not sure, but our next-door neighbors might have not evacuated like the rest of us.
7. You shouldn't have bought batteries for the flashlight. Now we won't be able to see in the dark.
8. TV weather forecasters must not have be given enough information about the storm. They didn't give people enough warning.
9. The Hamilton Bridge should be closed after the earthquake. Because it wasn't closed, there was a terrible accident and several people were killed.
10. Sally forgot to take her cat with her. She must have been left in a hurry.

NAME: ______________________________ DATE: ______________

UNIT 17 VOCABULARY EXERCISE

Read the speech. Then complete the sentences. Use the words in the box.

Ms. Garcia: Ladies and gentlemen, thank you for coming tonight. We're going to hear from a man who wants to be the next governor of New York—Mr. Alan Banks. Our question tonight is, "What is the most important problem in New York?"

Mr. Banks: The environment is our number-one problem. The people of New York want clean air and clean water. If you elect me, I will work hard to make New York clean again. New York needs cars that get forty miles to a gallon of gas. Big cars make our air dirty, and they use too much energy. I promise to give money back to people who buy small cars. People who drive big cars will pay a higher energy tax. The people of New York also want clean streets. There is too much trash on our streets. I promise to clean them up! The bottles, cans, and newspapers on our streets can be collected and used again. I say, "Let's get clean, New York!" Remember to vote on November 2nd.

cut taxes	litter	polling place	recycle
fuel-efficient	~~politician~~	pollute	vote

1. Mr. Banks is a ____politician____.
2. Mr. Banks is in favor of ____________________ cars.
3. Mr. Banks doesn't like big cars because they ____________________ the air.
4. Mr. Banks doesn't want to ____________________ for owners of big cars.
5. Mr. Banks wants to ____________________ bottles, cans, and newspapers.
6. The people of New York don't want ____________________ on their streets.
7. You can ____________________ for Mr. Banks if you live in New York.
8. Most people vote at a ____________________ in their neighborhood.

NAME: ______________________ DATE: ______________

UNIT 17 GRAMMAR EXERCISES

Grammar to Communicate 1: Adverb Clauses: Reason

A **Complete each sentence. Choose the correct main clause or adverb clause. Write the correct letter.**

1. You shouldn't complain about the government __d__
2. The politician wasn't well known ____
3. ____ your garbage bill must be very high.
4. ____ we are volunteering to pick up litter alongside the highway on Saturday.
5. ____ Norman quit working there.
6. The bus drivers are going on strike ____

a. because he hadn't given many speeches.
b. Since you don't recycle,
c. because they don't get paid enough.
d. since you don't vote.
e. Because we care about the environment,
f. Since the company was not very successful,

B **Combine the sentences. Use the words in parentheses. Put the adverb clause at the beginning of the sentence if the word in parentheses starts with a capital letter.**

1. The company closed the factory. The employees lost their jobs.
   The employees lost their jobs because the company closed the factory.
   (because)
2. Management has refused to give us a raise. We're going on strike.
   ____
   (Since)
3. The politician was popular. He said he would cut taxes.
   ____
   (because)
4. He doesn't pay much for gas. He drives a fuel-efficient car.
   ____
   (since)
5. We recycle almost everything. We think it will help the environment.
   ____
   (Because)
6. She doesn't vote. She doesn't think it would make much of a difference.
   ____
   (Since)

NAME: ______________________________ DATE: ______________

Grammar to Communicate 2: Adverb Clauses: Contrast

A **Complete the sentences. Circle the letter of the correct answer.**

1. Although my car is fuel-efficient,

   (**a.**) I pay over $100 a month on gas. **b.** gas isn't very expensive.

2. Even though everyone I know voted for Greg Bridges,

   a. he won. **b.** he didn't win.

3. The grass in my front yard is brown and dry, but

   a. I'm going to water it. **b.** I'm not going to water it.

4. Although I know big cars aren't good for the environment,

   a. I drive one. **b.** I don't drive one.

5. Although the air quality in my city keeps getting worse and worse,

   a. I've decided to move. **b.** I never want to leave.

6. Even though the water in the lake is a little polluted,

   a. we sometimes swim there. **b.** we never swim there.

B **Complete the sentences. Circle the correct answers.**

1. I buy that product, (**even though**) / **but** it has plastic packaging.
2. We could see the stars, **but / even though** there was a lot of pollution.
3. **Although / But** it takes more time to hang my clothes outside to dry, I like to do it because it saves electricity.
4. Air conditioners contribute to air pollution, **even though / but** we use them all summer long.
5. **But / Although** it takes longer to get to school, I usually walk there.
6. **Even though / But** I don't recycle, I admire people who do.
7. People eat fish from that lake, **even though / but** it is polluted!
8. Some scientists say our planet will be destroyed by global warming soon, **even though / but** I don't want to believe it.

NAME: ______________________________ DATE: ______________

Grammar to Communicate 3: *Because of / Despite / In Spite of*

A **Complete the sentences. Use *because, because of, despite,* or *in spite of.* More than one answer may be possible.**

1. I voted for the candidate because of his promise to cut taxes.
2. ___________ the hard work, many people go into politics.
3. ___________ he got the most votes, Mr. Potter became mayor.
4. Many candidates are elected ___________ people's belief that they are not totally honest.
5. Senator Jones won the election again ___________ we thought she did a wonderful job during her first term.
6. ___________ what you say, I'm not voting for that candidate.
7. I never vote for anyone ___________ his or her nice smile.

B **Rewrite the sentences in two ways. Use *despite* in the first sentence and *in spite of* in the second sentence.**

1. Even though the candidate has bad speaking skills, people like him.
   a. Despite the candidate's bad speaking skills, people like him.
   b. ______________________________
2. Although the weather is awful, many voters went to the polling stations.
   a. ______________________________
   b. ______________________________
3. Even though there was a long line, I waited to shake the candidate's hand.
   a. ______________________________
   b. ______________________________
4. Although people were angry at some of the president's bad decisions, he was elected again.
   a. ______________________________
   b. ______________________________

NAME: ______________________________ DATE: ______________

Review and Challenge

Complete the sentences. Circle the correct letter.

1. We take showers instead of baths ______ we can conserve more water that way.

   a. although **(b.)** because **c.** but **d.** even though

2. ______ she isn't a citizen, she couldn't vote in the election last week.

   a. Since **b.** Even though **c.** In spite of **d.** But

3. I take the bus to work Monday to Thursday, ______ I usually drive my car on Fridays.

   a. since **b.** because of **c.** but **d.** even though

4. I love to take long, hot baths, ______ I know I'm using more water than I should.

   a. because **b.** even though **c.** but **d.** in spite of

5. ______ the workers went on strike for over a month, the company refused to give them everything they were asking for.

   a. But **b.** Despite **c.** Because **d.** Although

6. ______ I could see oil in the water, I wouldn't let my children swim there.

   a. Because **b.** Because of **c.** Even though **d.** Despite

7. She won the election ______ the terrible story that the newspaper printed about her.

   a. in spite of **b.** because of **c.** but **d.** although

8. ______ the high cost of health insurance, most people buy it.

   a. Since **b.** Because of **c.** Even though **d.** Despite

9. The school closed ______ the teachers' strike.

   a. although **b.** because of **c.** since **d.** despite

10. I want to buy a new car, ______ I don't have enough money saved up yet.

    a. but **b.** even though **c.** because **d.** in spite of

NAME: ______________________ DATE: ____________

UNIT 18 VOCABULARY EXERCISE

Complete the paragraphs. Use the words in the boxes.

~~balance~~	costs	debt	interest	minimum payment	paid off

Charley used his credit cards a lot, and he got into trouble. Every month, he saw the balance (1.) on his credit card bill. It was getting higher and higher. He knew he was spending too much money, but he didn't care. After five years, his credit card bill was $50,000. Charley was in serious __________ (2.). How did this happen? Charley made some bad mistakes. His worst mistake? He never __________ (3.) the balance on his account. He always made the __________ (4.). Every month, the credit card company added __________ (5.) to the money Charley owed. Now Charley is in deep trouble. The interest __________ (6.) more than Charley's purchases.

approve	charges	deposits	due date	go below	mortgage

Zulma is careful with her credit card. She always pays on time. Her bill is paid by the __________ (7.). She pays off the balance, so she never has interest __________ (8.). Now Zulma wants to buy a house. Her credit is good, and she has saved a lot of money. The bank will probably __________ (9.) her loan. If she buys a home, she won't pay rent. She will pay a __________ (10.). Zulma is a good money manager. She keeps track of her checks and her __________ (11.). She likes to keep her checking account balance at $500, and she tries hard not to __________ (12.) that.

NAME: ______________________ DATE: ______________

UNIT 18 GRAMMAR EXERCISES

Grammar to Communicate 1: Present Real Conditionals

A **Complete each sentence. Circle the letter of the correct answer.**

1. ____ you should try to get a higher-paying job.

   a. If you get really good grades, (b.) If you need to earn more money,

2. You should get a student loan ____

   a. if you can't pay for your tuition. b. if you can't pay your mortgage.

3. ____ you can apply for a scholarship.

   a. If you get really good grades, b. If you need to earn more money,

4. ____ you should open an account at a different one.

   a. If you don't like your bank, b. If you can't pay off your credit card,

5. ____ you should consider a career in banking.

   a. If you have a credit card, b. If you love working with numbers,

B **Complete the sentences with the correct form of the verbs.**

1. If you ___see___ (see) a bank, please ___let___ (let) me know.
2. I __________ (worry) if the balance in my checking account __________ (go) below $500.
3. Many banks __________ (make) special offers if they __________ (look for) new customers.
4. If we __________ (have) any extra money at the end of the month, we __________ (put) it in our savings account.
5. If you __________ (keep) more than $500 in your savings account, the bank __________ (pay) you 1.5% interest.
6. The company __________ (charge) $50 if a customer __________ (not / pay) the minimum payment by the due date.
7. If you __________ (plan) to buy a new house, __________ (try) to put some money aside each month.

NAME: ______________________ DATE: ______________

Grammar to Communicate 2: Future Real Conditionals

A **Complete the sentences. Use the correct form of the verbs.**

1. If you ___open___ (open) an account here, we ___will give___ (give) you free checks.
2. If I __________ (give) the bank $20,000, how much __________ my monthly mortgage payment __________ (be)?
3. If I __________ (spend) all of my money this weekend, I __________ (not / have) enough for the rest of the month.
4. Our phone bill __________ (be) much less expensive if you __________ (stop) making so many long-distance calls.
5. You __________ (hurt) your credit if you __________ (miss) credit card payments.
6. If you __________ (not / have) enough to pay your rent this month, I __________ (lend) you some money.

B **Write statements or questions. Put the words in correct order. Use *if*.**

1. I / a cell phone / how much / get / cost / it / every month

   If I get a cell phone, how much will it cost every month?
2. we / pay / our mortgage / can't / we / ask / might / next month / for a loan

   ____
3. pay / $1,000 a month / we / how much / there / be / interest

   ____
4. put / in my savings account / extra / this month / I / money / have / I / it

   ____
5. do / can't / we / this month / pay / our bills / what / we

   ____

NAME: ______________________________ DATE: ______________

Grammar to Communicate 3: *If* and *When*

A **Complete the sentences. Use *if* or *when*.**

1. You'll be able to call home anytime ___when___ you get your new cell phone.
2. You can pay me back __________ you get your paycheck next week.
3. __________ I get the promotion I'm hoping for, I'll get a 20% raise!
4. I'd love to save some money. __________ I eat at home more often, it will be easy to put some money away.
5. The loan officer at the bank promised to call tomorrow, so I'll call you __________ I hear from him.
6. Many people get into debt __________ they use credit cards more often than cash. It has become a serious problem.
7. I'm not sure Tony is coming, but I'll tell him the news __________ I see him.

B **Complete the conversations. Use the words in parentheses. Add *if* or *when*.**

1. **A:** I got a job!

   B: Great news. ___When you start getting a paycheck___ (start getting a paycheck), you can start paying off your debt.

2. **A:** We found a house that we love, and we've applied for a mortgage.

   B: Good luck! ______________________________ (buy a house), you won't have to pay rent anymore.

3. **A:** I want to return these shoes, but I didn't keep the receipt.

   B: Most stores won't take back purchases ______________________________ (not / have the receipt).

4. **A:** I get very annoyed ______________________________ (people ask me about money).

   B: Well, ______________________________ (feel that way), I know that you're going to be very annoyed when you go to the bank tomorrow!

NAME: ______________________________ **DATE:** ______________

Review and Challenge

Find and correct the mistake in each item.

1. I won't be able to pay you back ~~when~~ if the bank doesn't approve my loan. They promised to call today.
2. My bank pays interest every month when customers will keep a balance of at least $500.
3. I won't go to the concert when the tickets are too expensive. I can't afford more than about $25.
4. If my boss won't give me a raise at the end of the year, I might start looking for a new job.
5. You should stop eating out so much if you'll want to save money.
6. If you're angry that Joe hasn't paid you back, you need to talk to him about it when you're seeing him.
7. We'll ask my parents for a loan if we need money for a new car. We're not sure we should ask them.
8. If you aren't going below the minimum balance, your checking account will be free.
9. Some advice for you: If you don't need something, won't buy it.
10. If someone will have a lot of debt, he or she probably doesn't sleep well at night.

NAME: ______________________________ **DATE:** ______________

UNIT 19 VOCABULARY EXERCISE

Complete the conversations. Use the words in the boxes.

break my heart	break up with	make up your mind	out of her hands	~~propose~~

1. **Victor:** Cheri, will you marry me?

   Cheri: Oh, Victor! I've been waiting for you to ____propose____!

2. **Eiko:** Let's go to a Japanese restaurant. Or maybe you prefer Thai food?

   Wang: I like both. Just __________________!

3. **Tom:** Is Yasmina still George's girlfriend?

   Nancy: Oh, no. She decided to __________________ him three weeks ago.

4. **Paulo:** I can't marry you. I love someone else.

   Carmen: No, Paulo, don't tell me that! Why do you want to __________________?

5. **Anna:** In the old days, a father decided on a husband for his daughter.

   Polly: Really? You mean the decision was __________________?

approve of	can't think straight	listen to my heart	is up to you

6. **Galina:** I don't like my sister's boyfriend.

   Ivan: What's wrong with him?

   Galina: I don't __________________ him because he is much older than she is.

7. **Elena:** Should we have our wedding reception at a restaurant or at a hotel?

   Carlos: I don't care, my love. It __________________.

8. **Isaac:** What's wrong with Benji?

   Roberto: He's in love! Don't ask him anything today. He __________________.

9. **Alice:** Are you going to marry Jean-Pierre?

Marie: No, I'm not.

Alice: Are you crazy? He's so handsome . . . and so rich!

Marie: But I don't love him, and I must ____________________.

NAME: ______________________ DATE: ____________

UNIT 19 GRAMMAR EXERCISES

Grammar to Communicate 1: Present Real and Unreal Conditionals

A **Complete each sentence. Circle the correct answer.**

1. If I were you, I **would / wouldn't** propose to Tanya tonight. She's too upset. Wait until tomorrow.
2. I don't want to hurt Jason. What would you say if you **wanted / didn't want** to break his heart?
3. If you didn't listen to your heart, you **would / wouldn't** regret it.
4. If you were really in love, you **would / wouldn't** be able to think straight.
5. If your parents **approved / didn't approve** of your boyfriend, would you break up with him?
6. She'd be able to make up her mind if she **knew / didn't know** all the facts.

B **Read each situation. Complete the sentences.**

1. I live in a very small apartment. I can't get a roommate.
   If I ___didn't live___ in such a small apartment, I ___could get___ a roommate.
2. My house is far from the subway. It's very cheap.
   If my house __________ closer to the subway, it __________ so cheap.
3. My neighbors are really noisy. I can't sleep at night.
   I __________ sleep at night if my neighbors __________ so noisy.
4. I never see my neighbors. I don't ask them to be quieter.
   If I __________ them, I __________ them to be quieter.
5. I love my apartment. I don't want to move.
   I __________ to move if I __________ my apartment.
6. It's a great apartment. But the neighbors are noisy.
   If the neighbors __________ so noisy, it __________ perfect.

NAME: ______________________ DATE: ____________

Grammar to Communicate 2: Making Wishes: Present and Future

A **Complete the sentences. Write *wish(es)* or *hope(s)* and the correct form of the verbs. Use the negative where necessary.**

1. I really ___hope___ you ___didn't spend___ (spend) too much on my birthday gift.
2. We __________ the bank __________ (approve) our loan soon.
3. Don't you __________ you __________ (have to) work?
4. Many people __________ that they __________ (win) the lottery, so they buy a ticket every day.
5. I really __________ I __________ (have) a lot of debt. The bank will never give me a loan.
6. What do you __________ that you __________ (be able to) change about your life?
7. Most people say they __________ they __________ (make) more money.

B **People are talking about their problems. What do they wish? Write sentences.**

1. My car uses a lot of gas.

   I wish my car didn't use a lot of gas.
2. My landlord raises my rent every year.

   ____
3. Living in the city is expensive.

   ____
4. My apartment isn't very nice.

   ____
5. I don't have a view.

   ____
6. I'm not good at saving money.

   ____

NAME: ______________________________ DATE: ______________

Grammar to Communicate 3: Unreal Past Conditionals

A **Read the situations. Then mark the sentences *T* (true) or *F* (false).**

1. If Julia had listened to her heart, she would have married Alberto.

   Julia loved Alberto. T

2. If we had known how unhappy Jon was, we wouldn't have told him to marry Lee.

   We thought Jon was happy. ____

3. If Teresa had really been in love, she wouldn't have been able to think straight.

   Teresa wasn't really in love. ____

4. If Mike's parents hadn't approved of Diana, he wouldn't have proposed to her.

   Mike's parents didn't approve of Diana. ____

5. Sue would have married Rick if she hadn't thought he was so irresponsible.

   Sue and Rick got married. ____

B **Complete the sentences. Use the correct form of the verbs in parentheses.**

1. If Ines hadn't moved (move) to New York, she and Peter would never have met.
2. Ines wouldn't have gone to the club that night if her friends ________ (insist).
3. She ________ (go) to bed early that night if she hadn't gone out with her friends.
4. If it ________ (be) a regular Saturday night, Ines would have gone to a movie.
5. She wouldn't have been interested in the club if her friends ________ (tell) her how much fun it was.
6. She would have gone to the club sooner if she ________ (hate) loud music.
7. What ________ (happen) in Ines and Peter's lives if they ________ (meet) that night so long ago?

NAME: ______________________________ DATE: ____________

Review and Challenge

Find the mistake in each item. Circle the letter and correct the mistake.

1. We want to go to the beach tomorrow. I wish (A) the weather (B) will (C) be (D) nice.

   Correct: hope

2. If I were (A) Ann, I (B) won't (C) go out (D) with Tim. But it's her decision.

   Correct: ______________________________

3. I wish I lived (A) in the city. If (B) I lived (C) there, I was (D) be able to make more money.

   Correct: ______________________________

4. I wish (A) I wasn't (B) so heavy. If I start (C) a diet this week, I might (D) be able to lose weight before the wedding.

   Correct: ______________________________

5. If it were (A) up to Carla's parents, she would break up (B) with Louis. But I know that it would break (C) his heart if she breaks up (D) with him.

   Correct: ______________________________

6. My girlfriend and I wouldn't (A) have met (B) if we hadn't (C) take (D) Mrs. Costa's English class.

   Correct: ______________________________

7. I wish I can (A) get a raise. If (B) I made (C) more money, I 'd propose (D) to my girlfriend.

   Correct: ______________________________

8. Why does Cara keep going out with Bill if she doesn't love (A) him? If I am (B) her, I'd (C) break up with him and find (D) a better boyfriend.

   Correct: ______________________________

9. If we would (A) had (B) a big wedding, it would have (C) been (D) very expensive.

   Correct: ______________________________

10. What do you think Sheila would say (A) when (B) Carlos proposed (C) to her? Would she say (D) yes or no?

    Correct: ______________________________

NAME: ______________________ DATE: ____________

UNIT 20 VOCABULARY EXERCISE

Look at the underlined words in the sentences. Match the underlined words with the phrasal verbs that have the same meaning. Write the correct letters.

__c__ **1.** Emma has decided to <u>cancel</u> the wedding.

____ **2.** I hope I don't <u>meet</u> anyone I know today. My hair looks terrible.

____ **3.** Rick didn't save his work on the computer, so he had to <u>write</u> the report <u>again</u>.

____ **4.** Michelle made a mistake in her checkbook. She asked the bank to help her <u>find</u> her mistake.

____ **5.** Federico didn't know the word *balloon.* He had to <u>find</u> it in the dictionary.

____ **6.** Bob wants to <u>go on a date with</u> Sarah.

____ **7.** Bill forgot to <u>give</u> his homework to the teacher.

____ **8.** Nikolai hopes his professor won't <u>ask</u> him <u>a question in class</u> today.

a. look up

b. figure out

c. call off

d. call on

e. run into

f. hand in

g. do over

h. take out

NAME: ______________________________ DATE: ______________

UNIT 20 GRAMMAR EXERCISES

Grammar to Communicate 1: Phrasal Verbs: Transitive and Intransitive

A **Underline the phrasal verbs. Mark the verbs *T* (transitive) or *I* (intransitive).**

A: Ted and I broke up (I) last night.

B: You're kidding. I always thought you two got along so well.

A: We did when we first started going out. But lately, I've been feeling like I can't count on him. And I was right! I got up early yesterday and called Ted. He didn't pick up his phone, so I went to the park without him. Then I ran into him at the park . . . with Joanne! So I told them off. Then I went home. And last night I e-mailed Ted and called off our engagement.

B: Well, you'll get over him soon. You put up with a lot of bad stuff from him. It's time to move on!

B **Complete the sentences. Use the phrasal verbs in the box.**

call off	call on	~~figure out~~	give up	make up	run into

1. I can't ___figure out___ why Liz is angry at me. What did I do?
2. I don't like it when teachers ______________ me. I can never think of what to say.
3. We had to ______________ the game because of the rain.
4. Don't ______________. If you work harder, you'll succeed.
5. I hope I don't ______________ anyone I know today. I look awful!
6. I'm sure you and Derek will ______________. You fight all the time, but you always work it out.

NAME: ______________________ DATE: ______________

Grammar to Communicate 2:
Phrasal Verbs: Separable and Inseparable

A **Complete the sentences with the correct particles. Use each of the following particles twice: *away*, *on*, and *up*. Then write *S* (separable) or *I* (inseparable) next to each sentence.**

1. S Are you really going to throw away those shoes? Someone might want them.
2. ____ I'm thinking of giving ________ my apartment and moving back to my parents' house.
3. ____ You didn't try ________ that sweater before you bought it, did you?
4. ____ Why don't we take ________ tennis? It's great exercise.
5. ____ I'd like you to empty the dishwasher and put the dishes ________.
6. ____ You know you can always count ________ your friends.

B **Underline the phrasal verb in the sentences. Then rewrite the sentences if possible. If the sentences can't be rewritten, write *inseparable* on the line.**

1. If we run out of cereal, we can send Geo to the store for more.
   inseparable
2. I wish you hadn't put off your homework until Sunday night.
   ____
3. Henry and Sally want to bring up their children in the city.
   ____
4. I was very surprised when Kathy showed up at the party last night.
   ____
5. Would you mind putting away your clean clothes?
   ____
6. Did Magda really turn down Peter's proposal?
   ____
7. I'd like to go over this month's budget because I'm worried.
   ____

NAME: ______________________ DATE: ______________

Grammar to Communicate 3: Phrasal Verbs with Pronouns

A **Match the sentences and the responses. Write the correct letters.**

__b__ **1.** What's the balance on your credit card?

____ **2.** Did you quit smoking?

____ **3.** Does Steve know about the surprise party we've planned for him tonight?

____ **4.** I can't find my red jacket.

____ **5.** Do you still have a cold?

a. Yes. I finally gave it up.

b. I don't have one. I paid it off.

c. Yes. I can't seem to get over it!

e. No. I don't think anyone has given it away.

f. I think you took it off in the dining room.

B **Complete the conversations. Read the questions. Complete the answers. Use a pronoun in your answers.**

1. A: What happened? Did Emma turn you down?

B: Yes, she did. She __turned me down__.

2. A: Have you picked up our clothes from the dry cleaner yet?

B: No. I haven't had time to ______________ yet.

3. A: Have you filled out the college application form yet?

B: Of course. I ______________ and mailed it yesterday.

4. A: Can we count on Molly to be on time?

B: Yes, we can always ______________ to be responsible.

5. A: Why don't I pick up you and Manny at 7:00?

B: Yes. Please ______________ at 7:00. We'd appreciate it.

6. A: Why do you put up with Joe? He's impossible!

B: I ______________ because I love him.

NAME: ______________________ DATE: ____________

Review and Challenge

Complete the conversation with the words in the box. Be careful. There are some extra words.

broke up	get over it	move on	ran into
called me back	give up	pick you up	~~show up~~
get along	make up	put off	take her out

Angel: Hey, Steve. Are you going to ___show up___ (1.) at Brian's party tonight?

Steve: Yes, I'll be there. Are you?

Angel: I want to go, but I don't have a ride.

Steve: I can take you. If you want, I can ______________ (2.) at around 7:30.

Angel: That would be great. By the way, did you hear that Brian and Katy ______________ (3.)?

Steve: Yes. I ______________ (4.) Brian yesterday at the mall, and he told me the news. It's pretty sad, but they just couldn't ______________ (5.). They were fighting all the time.

Angel: So I guess it was time for them to ______________ (6.). I hope they'll both ______________ (7.) soon.

Steve: Me, too. Hey, you've always liked Katy. Why don't you ______________ (8.)?

Angel: That's not a great idea. I called her a few times last year, but she never ______________ (9.). I finally had to ______________ (10.) calling her.

Answer Key

Unit 1, page 1, vocabulary

2. get a part
3. perform
4. be in the competition
5. win awards
6. appeared
7. direct

Unit 1, page 2, grammar

Grammar to Communicate 1

A

2. have performed
3. has appeared
4. received
5. didn't call
6. have known
7. have never been

B

1. made, was
2. practiced, was
3. has made, finished
4. have been, saw

Grammar to Communicate 2

A

1. was, has performed
2. joined, has played, has been
3. have been, got, have known
4. have met, were, started, have become

B

2. for
3. for, since
4. for
5. since
6. since
7. for

Grammar to Communicate 3

A

2. b
3. a
4. a
5. a

B

2. I have been OR I've been
3. did you go
4. I went
5. I was
6. was
7. I did
8. I saw
9. She has always been
10. Have you ever seen
11. I have seen

Review and Challenge

Thanks for your e-mail. It ~~has been~~ was good to hear from you. I ~~was~~ have been in New York ~~since~~ for the past two weeks. Our school's jazz band ~~was~~ has been in several competitions. Tonight is our last performance. I'm very excited about it.

We ~~had~~ have had a lot of fun since we got here. Yesterday we ~~have gone~~ went to the Museum of Modern Art. We ~~have seen~~ saw some really famous paintings. This morning we ~~have visited~~ visited the Empire State Building. I ~~have bought~~ bought you a souvenir Empire State Building keychain.

Unit 2, page 6, vocabulary

2. arthritis
3. have trouble sleeping
4. chicken pox
5. injury
6. diabetes
7. have a good appetite
8. vitamins
9. is acting up

Unit 2, page 8, grammar

Grammar to Communicate 1

A

2. has been studying
3. has been examining
4. has been complaining
5. haven't been crying
6. have been taking

B

1. haven't been eating
2. has been acting up, have been hurting
3. have been coughing, haven't been feeling
4. have been taking, have been making

Grammar to Communicate 2

A

2. has been taking / has taken
3. has been coughing
4. has been having
5. has gone / has been going
6. has been
7. hasn't been feeling
8. has been waiting
9. has been feeling
10. hasn't called

B

2. **A:** Have you ~~been finishing~~ finished last night's homework?
3. **A:** Have you ~~been going~~ gone to the hospital yet to see **Hannah** and her new baby?
4. **A:** That's good. I've been ~~being~~ a little worried about you.
5. **A:** Have you ever ~~been having~~ had the chicken pox?

Answer Key

Grammar to Communicate 3

A

2. the score is 4–4
3. every day this week
4. for about a year
5. every day
6. for almost an hour

B

2. How long have you studied at this school? / How long have you been studying at this school?
3. How many times have you gone to the doctor so far this year?
4. How much water have you drunk today?
5. How many colds have you had so far this year?
6. How long have you been working on this exercise?

Review and Challenge

Do you remember that I had a doctor's appointment last week? Well, I've just ~~been receiving~~ received an upsetting phone call. Dr. Grey's office called to tell me that my test results aren't very good. I was really surprised to hear this because I've been trying really hard to get in better shape. I've been eating healthier food, and I've ~~taken~~ been taking long walks several times a week. This week, I've ~~been taking~~ taken a walk every day!

The doctor says that I am 25 pounds overweight and that I might get diabetes! I can't believe it! But I have to believe it. After all, Dr. Grey has ~~been knowing~~ known me almost all my life. So I've ~~been deciding~~ decided to do something about it. I've gone through all the food in my kitchen, and I've thrown away all the junk food. And I've been calling health clubs for the past few hours. I haven't ~~been~~ found one yet, but I'll keep trying. Have you ever ~~been belonging~~ belonged to a gym? All the gyms I've called so far are really expensive!

Unit 3, page 12, vocabulary

A

2. victims
3. witness
4. suspects
5. questioned
6. investigated
7. detective

B

1. b
2. a
3. c
4. b

Unit 3, page 14, grammar

Grammar to Communicate 1

A

2. had felt
3. had never been
4. had been
5. had left
6. had arrived
7. had seen
8. had called
9. had gotten
10. had disappeared

B

2. The man had robbed two stores and three houses.
3. By Saturday night, the police had questioned four witnesses.
4. One witness had seen the suspect clearly.
5. The detectives had found the stolen money by Sunday night.

Grammar to Communicate 2

2. saw
3. hadn't noticed
4. hadn't gone
5. hadn't come
6. was
7. called
8. told
9. arrived
10. had discovered
11. also had taken
12. had had
13. had been
14. heard
15. had come
16. looked
17. had seen
18. remembered
19. had seen
20. had lived
21. was
22. had, become
23. gave
24. ran
25. had already driven
26. arrived
27. had already arreste

Grammar to Communicate 3

A

2. had been lying
3. were waiting
4. had been planning
5. was waiting
6. had been watching
7. had been trying
8. hadn't been working
9. were waiting
10. had been waiting
11. were expecting

B

2. got, had been watching
3. was watching, heard
4. was trying, screamed, called
5. arrested, had been breaking

Review and Challenge

2. C: arrested
3. D: broke
4. D: had gotten
5. D: came
6. A: were waiting
7. D: lost
8. C: had told
9. D: lived
10. A: had been living

Unit 4, page 18, vocabulary

2. garbage disposal
3. trash chute
4. superintendent
5. tenant
6. landlady / landlord
7. landlord / landlady
8. entrance
9. security guard

Unit 4, page 19, grammar

Grammar to Communicate 1

A

2. 2, 1
3. 2, 1
4. 1, 2
5. 1, 2

B

2. The
3. the
4. a
5. Ø
6. Ø
7. The
8. the
9. an
10. The
11. The
12. a
13. The
14. a

Grammar to Communicate 2

A

2. yes
3. no
4. no

B

2. an
3. a
4. the
5. the
6. a
7. any
8. some
9. a
10. the
11. a
12. the
13. the / some
14. some
15. the

Grammar to Communicate 3

A

2. Apartments are usually easier than houses.
3. In apartment buildings, superintendents do the tenants' repairs.
4. Houses are expensive to keep up.
5. When you live in an apartment, neighbors are always close by.

B

2. An
3. a
4. Ø
5. Ø
6. a, the
7. Ø
8. Ø, the, a

Review and Challenge

2. Do you know where ~~a~~ the superintendent is? He was supposed to be here an hour ago!
3. I want to buy some new curtains. I don't like ^the curtains I have now.
4. Let's meet at ~~a~~ the coffee shop on the ground floor of your building.
5. I think there might be ~~the~~ an apartment available next month.
6. I don't have ~~some~~ any extra keys for my apartment. Can you make one for me later today?
7. ~~A~~ The dishwasher isn't working, and the garbage disposal is making a terrible noise.
8. ~~A p~~ Parking is sometimes hard to find in my neighborhood.
9. Tenants pay rent, and ~~the~~ landlords should take care of their buildings.
10. Peter has ~~the~~ very noisy neighbors.

Unit 5, page 23, vocabulary

2. a
3. g
4. f
5. i
6. b
7. e
8. j
9. c
10. h

Unit 5, page 24, grammar

Grammar to Communicate 1

A

2. didn't you?
3. can he?
4. aren't you?
5. doesn't it?
6. have you?
7. isn't he?
8. will she?

B

2. You've interviewed more than one applicant for the job, haven't you?
3. There's another applicant waiting in the reception area, isn't there?
4. You should spend more than five minutes with each applicant, shouldn't you?
5. You told the receptionist to offer the applicants coffee, didn't you?
6. You'll make your decision by the end of the week, won't you?

Grammar to Communicate 2

A

2. So
3. too
4. Neither
5. either

Answer Key

B

2. I don't either.
3. Neither is mine.
4. Neither have I.
5. I am, too.
6. Mine does, too.
7. So are mine.
8. I didn't either.

Grammar to Communicate 3

A

2. either, or
3. both, and
4. neither, nor
5. both, and
6. either, or

B

2. are
3. is
4. is
5. have
6. thinks

Review and Challenge

2. A: I'll have Friday nights off, ~~haven't~~ won't I?
   B: Yes.
3. A: You couldn't drive me to the airport tomorrow, ~~couldn't~~ could you?
   B: Sorry, I'll be busy then.
4. A: They offered you the job, ~~did~~ didn't they?
   B: Yes.
5. A: I didn't get a copy of the company's policies.
   B: I didn't ~~neither~~ either.
6. A: Either a college degree or a lot of experience ~~are~~ is needed to get that job.
   B: Really?
7. A: I want to either work for a large international company ~~and~~ or start my own business. I can't decide.
   B: That's a tough decision.
8. A: Both talent and creativity ~~is~~ are required for this position.
   B: Well, I'm talented and creative!
9. A: Jane has a great personality, ~~does~~ doesn't she?
   B: Oh, yes. She's a wonderful person.
10. A: You aren't going to be here tomorrow, ~~will~~ are you?
    B: No. I have to visit my mother.

Unit 6, page 28, vocabulary

2. fry
3. marinate
4. broil
5. invented
6. cultivate
7. consume
8. steam
9. create

Unit 6, page 29, grammar

Grammar to Communicate 1

A

2. is marinated
3. are added, is eaten
4. are baked
5. is sold
6. are made, are eaten

B

2. Eggs are often boiled.
3. Steak is usually broiled.
4. Celery is hardly ever served hot.
5. Mushrooms are often sautéd with onions.
6. Pasta is almost always served with sauce.
7. Muffins are always baked in the oven.
8. Peanuts are usually grown in warm places.

Grammar to Communicate 2

A

2. wasn't, was
3. were, weren't, were
4. was
5. were, were
6. was

B

2. Spinach was introduced to Europe thousands of years ago by the Moors.
3. The early European settlers were taught how to grow corn by Native Americans.
4. In the 1500s, new foods were brought from the Americas to Europe by explorers.
5. Tomatoes were first grown in South America.
6. Tomatoes weren't eaten in England until the 1700s.

Grammar to Communicate 3

A

2. are cut up
3. stir-fry
4. call
5. is used
6. don't cook

B

2. was opened
3. sold
4. joined
5. wasn't liked
6. started
7. bought
8. began
9. offer
10. are sold

Answer Key

Review and Challenge

2. A warm climate is ~~need~~ needed to grow pineapples.
3. Many kinds of fruit ~~is~~ are cultivated in Hawaii.
4. How many hamburgers are ~~sell~~ sold in the U.S. every day?
5. Some kinds of meat are not eaten ~~from~~ by most people in my country.
6. Don't eat that apple until it's ~~washing~~ washed.
7. Before refrigeration, people ~~are~~ used salt to keep food fresh.
8. A lot of olive oil ~~are~~ is exported by Spain and Italy.
9. Many kinds of foods ~~are~~ were brought to Asia from the New World in the 1500s.
10. Corn was eaten ~~by people~~ in Mexico thousands of years ago.

Unit 7, page 33, vocabulary

2. are evacuating
3. have posted
4. clear
5. are searching
6. disappeared
7. are inspecting
8. replace

Unit 7, page 34, grammar

Grammar to Communicate 1

A

2. have been installed
3. has been hit
4. have been told, has been called
5. has been reported
6. has been closed, have been started

B

2. More than 300 people have been forced to leave their homes by the fire.
3. ——
4. Several elderly people have been rescued.
5. More than fifty people have been taken to the hospital.
6. The neighborhood has been called a disaster area.

Grammar to Communicate 2

2. need to be covered, needs to be brought
3. needs to be posted
4. needs to be evacuated
5. needs to be called
6. doesn't need to be held
7. need to be changed
8. need to be inspected
9. don't need to be told
10. need to be rescued
11. needs to be repaired, needs to be replaced
12. don't need to be locked

Grammar to Communicate 3

A

2. Central Park is being cleaned up.
3. Healthier food is being served for lunch.
4. Students are being taught how to eat better.
5. Classes for new parents are being held. / Classes are being held for new parents.
6. High school students are being hired to post signs.

B

2. are being checked
3. are being inspected
4. are being cleaned
5. are being replaced
6. are being fixed
7. are being installed
8. is organizing

Review and Challenge

A: I think the sprinkler system needs to ~~check~~ be checked. No one has ~~been~~ looked at it for a long time.

B: That's true. It ~~need~~ needs to be checked at least once a year. I'll call the company today.

A: Thanks. And what about the smoke alarms? ~~Has~~ Have the batteries been replaced recently?

B: Not really. The building is being cleaned this week. I'll ask the janitor to replace the batteries in all the smoke alarms.

A: And what about the lights in the stairs? Do some of those light bulbs need to ~~replace~~ be replaced, too?

B: No. After the accident, we ~~are~~ removed all the old bulbs and put in new ones.

A: Accident? What accident? What ~~was~~ happened?

B: A man fell because the light between the first and second floors was out. The light bulb needed to be replaced, but we didn't know about it until it was too late.

A: That's terrible. Well, the building is ~~been~~ being inspected next Monday. Let's take care of all these safety things.

Answer Key

Unit 8, page 38, vocabulary

2. exhausted
3. annoyed
4. refreshing
5. amazed
6. satisfying
7. advertisements
8. channel
9. commercials

Unit 8, page 39, grammar

Grammar to Communicate 1

A

1. satisfied
2. refreshing, energized
3. exhausting, tired, amazed
4. annoying, exciting, exciting

B

2. amazing, amazed
3. bored, boring
4. satisfying, satisfied

Grammar to Communicate 2

A

2. such
3. so
4. so
5. such
6. so
7. such
8. so

B

2. The potato chips in the ad looked so good that I went out and bought some.
3. That brand of jeans is so nice that I've decided to buy a pair next week.
4. The car in the commercial is so fast that it looks like it's flying.
5. It was such a long commercial that the company had to shorten it by 30 seconds.
6. It looks like such a great restaurant that we're eating there on Saturday night.
7. It's such a sad commercial that it made me cry.

Grammar to Communicate 3

A

2. small Japanese sports
3. cute little French
4. beautiful white wedding
5. tall pretty young
6. ugly old wood
7. lovely new beach

B

2. The model in the commercial had straight long brown hair.
3. The flower shop uses beautiful red roses.
4. How many commercials has that handsome young actor made?
5. That wonderful Spanish department store is huge.

Review and Challenge

2. That movie was so ~~bored~~ boring that I almost fell asleep twice.
3. The actor's voice was ~~such~~ so annoying that I turned off the TV and went to bed.
4. Studying for exams is really ~~exhausted~~ exhausting.
5. That cake looks so delicious ~~than~~ that I have to have a piece.
6. You have ~~so~~ such beautiful children.
7. My ~~black new~~ new black boots are so comfortable that I want to wear them every day.
8. My new electric pencil sharpener is ~~so~~ such a convenient tool.
9. Some ads are so bad that they're ~~embarrassed~~ embarrassing.
10. These ~~picnic plastic~~ plastic picnic plates were really cheap.

Unit 9, page 43, vocabulary

2. instruction manual
3. electricity
4. assemble
5. gadgets
6. engine
7. tools
8. useless
9. toolbox

Unit 9, page 44, grammar

Grammar to Communicate 1

A

2. that toasts bread
3. that help people see
4. who understands cars
5. that curls your hair
6. who fixes appliances
7. that opens bottles

B

2. The company that / which installs the best alarm systems is called StaySafe.
3. People who / that love to cook buy all the newest kitchen gadgets.
4. The neighbors who / that moved often lent me their tools.
5. The lawn mower that / which is in our garage belongs to our old neighbors.
6. The hammer that / which is in my toolbox also belongs to them.

Grammar to Communicate 2

A

2. Many people buy things which they don't really need.
3. She is the person who I call when I need advice.
4. They're the friends that I've known the longest.
5. I want those lights that you turn on and off by clapping your hands.
6. I want a toolbox which I can carry easily.

B

2. I bought a phone that / which is also a camera.
3. My friend got a new laptop that / which can burn CDs.
4. —
5. —
6. —
7. This is a device that / which makes my life much easier.
8. Do you know anyone who can fix my computer?

Grammar to Communicate 3

A

2. I couldn't afford any of the appliances that / which I looked at.
3. The salesperson who / that I talked to was not helpful.
4. I was disappointed by the products that / which I saw.
5. This is the store that / which my neighbor told me about.
6. It's a place that / which he had heard about from his boss.
7. This neighbor is someone who / that I may never speak to again.

B

2. Who is the salesperson you were talking to?
3. Which is the dishwasher you were looking at?
4. Did you see the great flashlight I told you about?
5. Is this the device you were looking for?

Review and Challenge

2. The people ^(who / that) live next door to us have a garage full of strange gadgets.
3. Do you know anyone ~~which~~ (who / that) can fix my dishwasher?
4. I got my refrigerator at the appliance store that ~~it~~ just opened on Main Street.
5. We have all the appliances we need ~~them~~.
6. Were you satisfied with the salesperson you spoke to ~~him~~?
7. Why did you buy something you didn't need ~~it~~?
8. There are a lot of people ~~which~~ (who / that) love gadgets, but I'm not one of them.
9. I saw an ad for a pen that ~~write~~ (writes) in ten different colors.
10. The store at the mall ^(that / which) has the best prices is probably Gears Department Store.

Unit 10, page 48, vocabulary

A

2. rain check
3. try on
4. fitting room
5. exchange
6. refund

B

1. wonder
2. find out
3. has been in business
4. restroom

Unit 10, page 50, grammar

Grammar to Communicate 1

A

2. I don't know <u>when the next bus will be here.</u>
3. I'm afraid <u>that we are all sold out of that item.</u>
4. I'm glad <u>you checked the size before you bought it.</u>
5. I'm sorry <u>that shirt didn't fit you.</u>
6. I'm not sure <u>where the post office is.</u>
7. I wonder <u>when the sale ends.</u>

B

2. b
3. a
4. d
5. c
6. d
7. a

Grammar to Communicate 2

A

2. Can you tell me where you got your jeans?
3. Do you know what time the store closes?
4. Could you tell me how much this sweater costs?
5. Do you remember what size he wears?

B

2. how much these gloves are? / how much these gloves cost?
3. where I can find a restroom?
4. why the restroom is closed?
5. what time it is?

Answer Key

Grammar to Communicate 3

A

2. the store will allow you to return shoes
3. we / I have this / that sweatshirt in a large
4. they gave me a receipt for those / these pants
5. you have time to try on this / that shirt before the store closes
6. the store had this / that skirt in other colors

B

2. I can't remember whether I paid with cash or with a credit card. / I can't remember whether I paid with a credit card or with cash.
3. Do you know if there's a payphone nearby?
4. I don't know if these shoes will be very comfortable.
5. I'm not sure whether this color will match my skirt.

Review and Challenge

2. D: the cosmetic department is
3. C: bought / had bought
4. C: got
5. D: sells
6. B: if / whether
7. D: these sunglasses cost
8. C: have
9. C: the new store will
10. D: .

Unit 11, page 54, vocabulary

A

2. financial aid
3. live on campus
4. dormitory
5. move in

B

1. give my notice
2. salary requirements

Unit 11, page 55, grammar

Grammar to Communicate 1

A

2. he'd / he had already done his homework.
3. Sam could help Yolanda write her résumé.
4. he was too tired to go to class today.
5. they were looking for a two-bedroom apartment.
6. she loved living on campus.
7. she'd try to live on campus next year

B

2. said
3. said
4. told
5. told
6. said

Grammar to Communicate 2

A

2. The interviewer asked me what skills I had.
3. The interviewer asked me how I had heard about the job.
4. The interviewer asked me when I had finished high school.
5. The interviewer asked me why I didn't have a résumé.

B

2. "Where did you go to college?"
3. "Why did you leave your last job?"
4. "How far away do you live from the office?"
5. "When can you start the job?'

Grammar to Communicate 3

A

2. c 3. a 4. b

B

2. if / whether the campus bus was usually on time
3. if / whether many students had been given financial aid this year
4. if / whether I was taking more than three classes
5. if / whether I had found a roommate
6. if / whether I was going to get a part-time job
7. if / whether I would be in class today

Review and Challenge

2. Emma told me her interview yesterday ~~went~~ had gone very well.
3. Marla asked me if I ~~am~~ was interested in studying with her tonight.
4. Regis said that the program ~~will~~ would accept more international students.
5. Jack told the interviewer he ~~was~~ had been at his old job for two years.
6. Crystal said she ~~is~~ was sorry for making so much noise last night.
7. The teacher ~~said~~ told us there would be a test on Friday.
8. Audrey ~~told~~ said she was going to live off campus next year.
9. He asked whether I ~~can~~ could start the job on April 1st.
10. I asked the cashier how late ~~did~~ the bookstore stayed open.

Answer Key

Unit 12, page 59, vocabulary

2. has trouble
3. postpones
4. wastes time
5. succeed in
6. socializes
7. be capable of
8. be curious
9. can't help

Unit 12, page 60, grammar

Grammar to Communicate 1

A

2. Having a lot of friends
3. Getting along with people
4. Not treating others badly
5. Trying to be kind
6. Not hating anyone

B

2. Spending time with friends after class is fun.
3. Working in pairs with people you don't know well is hard.
4. Working with someone I don't know bothers me.
5. Asking each other questions about the new grammar is helpful.
6. Making grammar mistakes sometimes doesn't bother me.

Grammar to Communicate 2

A

2. of
3. in
4. in
5. of
6. in
7. with

B

2. He learns new vocabulary by writing it in his notebook.
3. Gonzalo never succeeds at finishing anything on time.
4. The poor guy isn't capable of sitting in one place for a long time.
5. He gets tired of working on the same thing very quickly.
6. I take great pride in helping my friend improve his English.

Grammar to Communicate 3

A

1. breaking up
2. doing, making
3. being, spending

B

2. talking on the phone.
3. going out with friends.
4. meeting new people.
5. not being with other people.
6. thinking of ways to make friends.
7. talking to strangers.
8. making plans to socialize.

Review and Challenge

2. In fact, she can't stand ~~speak~~ speaking / to speak in public.
3. She is very good ~~in~~ at helping people find solutions to their problems.
4. ~~No~~ Not having any friends can be very difficult for children.
5. Many children have trouble ~~to socialize~~ socializing with others.
6. ~~Play~~ Playing with children their own age is a real problem for many.
7. Parents need to help their children understand that learning to get along with other kids ~~are~~ is very important.
8. Mihoko enjoys ~~helps~~ helping parents help their children.
9. Working with children ~~are~~ is her job—and her love.
10. She spends a lot of time ~~help~~ helping kids, and she loves doing it.

Unit 13, page 64, vocabulary

2. didn't mind
3. refused
4. convince
5. promised
6. warned
7. expected
8. pretended
9. managed

Unit 13, page 65, grammar

Grammar to Communicate 1

A

2. b
3. b
4. c
5. a
6. c

B

2. didn't use to have
3. used to take
4. aren't used to shopping
5. aren't used to living
6. am not used to taking

Answer Key

Grammar to Communicate 2

A

2. I
3. I
4. G
5. I
6. GI
7. I

B

2. to run
3. to call
4. waiting
5. to do
6. to be / being
7. to know
8. to register
9. having to

Grammar to Communicate 3

A

2. her class
3. Marsha
4. you
5. her
6. me
7. him

B

2. Maureen's best friend encouraged her not to make her decision too quickly.
3. Carlos's teacher wanted him to correct the errors in his paper.
4. Susana's mother reminded her to learn to be independent before she gets married.
5. Our grandparents asked us not to move too far away.
6. Tom expected me to be very successful.

Review and Challenge

2. Ginny and Tom decided ~~to not~~ not to get married until next year.
3. My new job is difficult, but I'm getting ~~use~~ used to it.
4. The teacher asked ~~he~~ him again and again to please be quiet.
5. I ~~use~~ used to take the bus to school, but now I carpool with my friend.
6. Karl is used to ~~stay~~ staying up until midnight to study.
7. I really dislike ~~to sit~~ sitting in the back of the class.
8. Patty's mother advised her not ~~taking~~ to take too many difficult classes.
9. She promised ~~practicing~~ to practice the piano every day.
10. ~~I'm~~ I used to belong to the school swim team, but I don't anymore.

Unit 14, page 69, vocabulary

2. g
3. e
4. b
5. f
6. h
7. a
8. c

Unit 14, page 70, grammar

Grammar to Communicate 1

A

2. D: ?
3. B: not
4. B: get
5. B: don't we
6. C: to celebrate
7. A: Why don't I

B

2. Why don't I
3. Let's
4. Why don't we
5. Let's not
6. Why don't we
7. Let me

Grammar to Communicate 2

A

2. would rather
3. would rather, would prefer
4. would prefer
5. would rather
6. Would, prefer, would, rather

B

2. Would you rather play tennis or go swimming?
3. Would you rather have a small party or invite all your friends?
4. Would you rather go out to a restaurant or get take-out?
5. Would you prefer to socialize with friends on Saturday night or stay home alone?
6. Would you prefer to watch TV or read a good book?
7. Would you prefer to play word games or sports?
8. Would you prefer to spend time with new friends or old friends?

Grammar to Communicate 3

A

2. Would you mind letting me use your phone?
3. Would you mind opening the door for me?
4. Would you mind driving me to class tomorrow?
5. Would you mind handing me that pen?
6. Would you mind helping me with this grammar?

B

2. Erin, would you mind putting the new books on the shelf?
3. Will, would you mind turning on the lights?
4. Joanne, would you mind closing the windows?
5. Walter, would you mind collecting the students' homework?

6. Bob, would you mind helping me take my things to my car?

Review and Challenge

2. Why don't I ~~carrying~~ carry your books for you?
3. Would you mind ~~to take~~ taking my coat?
4. We'd rather ~~to~~ have brunch on Saturday.
5. Would you prefer to walk to the store or ~~to~~ drive?
6. Would you mind giving me a ride? ~~Yes~~ No, I'd be happy to.
7. Let's ~~to~~ stay home tonight.
8. Why don't we see a movie tonight.?
9. Would you rather go skiing or ~~going~~ ice-skating?
10. Let me ~~helps~~ help Jimmy with his homework.

Unit 15, page 74, vocabulary

A

2. walk signal
3. crosswalk
4. right lane
5. left lane
6. parallel park
7. intersection

B

1. b
2. a
3. c

Unit 15, page 75, grammar

Grammar to Communicate 1

A

2. We ought to start looking for a gas station.
3. We ought to pull over.
4. You shouldn't drive above 30 mph here.
5. You ought to drive at least 55 mph on the highway.
6. What time should we leave the house?
7. You shouldn't drive your car into the city.

B

2. 'd better stop
3. 'd better pull over
4. 'd better not go
5. 'd better not throw
6. 'd better mail

Grammar to Communicate 2

A

2. 're not supposed to make
3. 'm not supposed to pass
4. 're not supposed to use
5. are supposed to stop

B

1. has to
2. can't, has to, has to, can't
3. can't, have to
4. can't, don't have to
5. have to, don't have to

Grammar to Communicate 3

A

2. didn't have to
3. were supposed to
4. did you have to
5. wasn't supposed to
6. wasn't supposed to

B

2. were supposed to
3. didn't have to
4. were supposed to
5. had to
6. didn't have to

Review and Challenge

2. We were supposed ^to take our road test yesterday, but we forgot.
3. ~~You~~ You'd better slow down on Main Street.
4. We can't ~~to~~ turn here.
5. You didn't ~~had~~ have to tell me to slow down.
6. I ~~haven't~~ didn't have to drive at all yesterday.
7. You'd better ~~no~~ not go over the speed limit downtown.
8. ~~I'm~~ I was supposed to study for my road test last night, but I had no time.
9. The city should ~~has~~ have more parking garages.
10. We ~~ought~~ should not pull over here.

Unit 16, page 79, vocabulary

2. predict
3. stock up on
4. flashlight
5. loses power
6. board up
7. blow away
8. flood
9. destroyed

Answer Key

Unit 16, page 80, grammar

Grammar to Communicate 1

A

2. should have bought
3. shouldn't have waited
4. should have taken
5. should have gotten
6. shouldn't have wasted

B

2. They shouldn't have gone to the beach on the morning of the storm.
3. They should have checked that they had a flashlight and batteries.
4. They should have bought candles.
5. They shouldn't have ignored all the warnings.
6. They should have believed the forecasters.

Grammar to Communicate 2

A

2. might not have had / may not have had
3. might have gone / may have gone
4. might have left / may have left
5. might have forgotten / may have forgotten

B

2. They may not have listened to the weather forecast.
3. They may have been out all day.
4. They might have come home earlier in the day.
5. They might have decided to drive to the city.
6. They might have made the wrong decision.

Grammar to Communicate 3

A

2. must have been
3. must have felt
4. must have gone
5. must have called
6. must have been sent

B

2. People must not have thought they were going to survive.
3. The emergency phone lines must have been busy all night.
4. Many people must have been taken to the hospital.
5. The fire department must have had to use all their trucks.
6. The city must have been a very frightening place.

Review and Challenge

2. The power must ~~to~~ have gone out while we were out.
3. He may have ~~went~~ gone to stay with his parents for a few days.
4. The fire ~~might~~ must have been put out.
5. It must ~~has~~ have been terrifying!
6. I'm not sure, but our next-door neighbors might ~~have not~~ not have evacuated like the rest of us.
7. You ~~shouldn't~~ should have bought batteries for the flashlight.
8. TV weather forecasters must not have ~~be~~ been given enough information about the storm.
9. The Hamilton Bridge should ~~be~~ have been closed after the earthquake.
10. She must have ~~been~~ left in a hurry.

Unit 17, page 84, vocabulary

2. fuel-efficient
3. pollute
4. cut taxes
5. recycle
6. litter
7. vote
8. polling place

Unit 17, page 85, grammar

Grammar to Communicate 1

A

2. a
3. b
4. e
5. f
6. c

B

2. Since management has refused to give us a raise, we're going on strike.
3. The politician was popular because he said he would cut taxes.
4. He doesn't pay much for gas since he drives a fuel-efficient car.
5. Because we think it will help the environment, we recycle almost everything.
6. Since she doesn't think it would make much of a difference, she doesn't vote.

Grammar to Communicate 2

A

2. b
3. b
4. a
5. b
6. a

B

2. even though
3. Although
4. but
5. Although
6. Even though
7. even though
8. but

Grammar to Communicate 3

A

2. Despite / In spite of
3. Because
4. despite / in spite of
5. because
6. Despite / In spite of
7. because of

B

1. b. In spite of the candidate's bad speaking skills, people like him.
2. a. Despite the awful weather, many voters went to the polling stations.
   b. In spite of the awful weather, many voters went to the polling stations.
3. a. Despite the long line, I waited to shake the candidate's hand.
   b. In spite of the long line, I waited to shake the candidate's hand.
4. a. Despite the president's bad decisions, he was elected again.
   b. In spite of the president's bad decisions, he was elected again.

Review and Challenge

2. a
3. c
4. b
5. d
6. a
7. a
8. d
9. b
10. a

Unit 18, page 89, vocabulary

2. debt
3. paid off
4. minimum payment
5. interest
6. costs
7. due date
8. charges
9. approve
10. mortgage
11. deposits
12. go below

Unit 18, page 90, grammar

Grammar to Communicate 1

A

2. a
3. a
4. a
5. b

B

2. worry, goes
3. make, are looking for
4. have, put
5. keep, pays
6. charges, doesn't pay
7. plan, try

Grammar to Communicate 2

A

2. give, will, be
3. spend, won't have
4. will be, stop
5. will hurt, miss
6. don't have, will lend

B

2. We might ask for a loan if we can't pay our mortgage next month. / If we can't pay our mortgage next month, we might ask for a loan.
3. How much interest will there be if we pay $1,000 a month? / If we pay $1,000 a month, how much interest will there be?
4. If I have extra money this month, I'll put it in my savings account.
5. What will we do if we can't pay our bills this month? / If we can't pay our bills this month, what will we do?

Grammar to Communicate 3

A

2. when
3. If
4. If
5. when
6. when
7. if

B

2. When you buy a house
3. if you don't have the receipt
4. when people ask me about money, if you feel that way

Review and Challenge

2. My bank pays interest every month when customers ~~will keep~~ keep a balance of at least $500.
3. I won't go to the concert ~~when~~ if the tickets are too expensive.
4. If my boss ~~won't~~ doesn't give me a raise at the end of the year, I might start looking for a new job.
5. You should stop eating out so much if ~~you'll~~ you want to save money.
6. If you're angry that Joe hasn't paid you back, you need to talk to him about it when ~~you're seeing~~ you see him.
7. ~~We'll~~ We might ask my parents for a loan if we need money for a new car.
8. If you ~~aren't going~~ don't go below the minimum balance, your checking account will be free.
9. Some advice for you: If you don't need something, ~~won't~~ don't buy it.
10. If someone ~~will have~~ has a lot of debt, he or she probably doesn't sleep well at night.

Answer Key

Unit 19, page 94, vocabulary

2. make up your mind
3. break up with
4. break my heart
5. out of her hands
6. approve of
7. is up to you
8. can't think straight
9. listen to my heart

Unit 19, page 96, grammar

Grammar to Communicate 1

A

2. didn't want
3. would
4. wouldn't
5. didn't approve
6. knew

B

2. were, wouldn't be
3. could, weren't
4. saw, would ask / 'd ask
5. would want / 'd want, didn't love
6. weren't, would be

Grammar to Communicate 2

A

2. hope, approves / will approve
3. wish, didn't have to
4. hope, will win
5. wish, didn't have
6. wish, were able to
7. wish, made

B

2. I wish my landlord didn't raise my rent every year.
3. I wish living in the city weren't expensive.
4. I wish my apartment were nice.
5. I wish I had a view.
6. I wish I were good at saving money.

Grammar to Communicate 3

A

2. T
3. T
4. F
5. F

B

2. hadn't insisted
3. would have gone
4. had been
5. hadn't told
6. hadn't hated
7. would have happened, hadn't met

Review and Challenge

2. C: wouldn't
3. D: would
4. B: weren't
5. D: broke up
6. D: taken
7. A: could
8. B: were
9. A: had
10. B: if

Unit 20, page 100, vocabulary

2. e
3. g
4. b
5. a
6. h
7. f
8. d

Unit 20, page 101, grammar

Grammar to Communicate 1

A

B: You're kidding. I always thought you two got along so well.

A: We did when we first started going out. But lately I've been feeling like I can't count on him. And I was right! I got up early yesterday and called Ted. He didn't pick up his phone, so I went to the park without him. Then I ran into him at the park . . . with Joanne! So, I told them off. Then I went home. And last night I e-mailed Ted and called off our engagement.

B: Well, you'll get over him soon. You put up with a lot of bad stuff from him. It's time to move on!

B

2. call on
3. call off
4. give up
5. run into
6. make up

Grammar to Communicate 2

A

2. S, up
3. S, on
4. I, up
5. S, away
6. I, on

B

2. put off, I wish you hadn't put your homework off until Sunday night.
3. bring up, Henry and Sally want to bring their children up in the city.
4. showed up, inseparable
5. putting away, Would you mind putting your clean clothes away?
6. turn down, Did Magda really turn Peter's proposal down?
7. go over, inseparable

Grammar to Communicate 3

A

2. a
3. e
4. f
5. c

B

2. pick them up
3. filled it out
4. count on her
5. pick us up
6. put up with him

Review and Challenge

2. pick you up
3. broke up
4. ran into
5. get along
6. move on
7. get over it
8. take her out
9. called me back
10. give up